REALMS
OF THE
EARTH
ANGELS

OTHER HAY HOUSE BOOKS
BY DOREEN VIRTUE, PH.D.

REALMS OF THE EARTH ANGELS

More Information for Incarnated Angels, Elementals, Wizards, and Other Lightworkers

Doreen Virtue, Ph.D.

HAY HOUSE, INC.
Carlsbad, California
London • Sydney • Johannesburg
Vancouver • Hong Kong • New Delhi

Copyright © 2007 by Doreen Virtue

Published and distributed in the United States by: Hay House, Inc.: www.hayhouse.com • **Published and distributed in Australia by:** Hay House Australia Pty. Ltd.: www.hayhouse. com.au • **Published and distributed in the United Kingdom by:** Hay House UK, Ltd.: www.hayhouse.co.uk • **Published and distributed in the Republic of South Africa by:** Hay House SA (Pty), Ltd.: orders@psdprom.co.za • **Distributed in Canada by:** Raincoast: www.raincoast.com • **Published in India by:** Hay House Publishers India: www.hayhouseindia.co.in

Editorial supervision: Jill Kramer • *Design:* Tricia Breidenthal

Library of Congress Control Number: 2006931627

ISBN: 978-1-4019-1718-0

10 09 08 07   5 4 3 2
1st edition, February 2007
2nd edition, February 2007

Printed in the United States of America

Contents

A Gentle Note to the Reader vii

Chapter 1:   Are You an Earth Angel? 1

Chapter 2:   Incarnated Angels. 25

Chapter 3:   Incarnated Elementals 61

Chapter 4:   Starpeople 91

Chapter 5:   The Wise Ones: Reincarnated
Sorceresses, High-Priestesses,
Sorcerers, Wizards, Shamans,
and Witches. 115

Chapter 6:   Blended Realms and Hybrids:
Mystic Angels, Knights,
Leprechauns, and Merpeople 141

Chapter 7:   If You Feel That You Fit into
Several Realms 165

Afterword: We're Counting on You! 179

Resources for Earth Angels 187

About the Author 193

A Gentle Note
to the Reader

*T*his is not your average book of angel stories, nor is it a book about angels in the
ordinary sense of the word. While people
usually think of Earth Angels as do-gooders,
this work takes the term literally, as you'll
soon see. The material within these pages
may surprise or even shock those of you who
are accustomed to a more mainstream view
of angels.

Some people may mistake this book's
intention, thinking that it supports the idea
of separation into groups. Yet, what I'm pre-
senting here is merely a description of the
personality-related, behavioral, and physical
characteristics of Earth Angels, similar to the

type of information found in astrology books. Those who are Earth Angels will relate to the concepts in this book; however, others may misunderstand or even object to what I'm offering here. My intention is to help and to heal, but sometimes such actions create controversy.

🔺 🔺 🔺

Ever since my book *Earth Angels* was first published in 2002, I've had the opportunity to talk to many people about the material. In my certification programs, I discuss the realms in depth and even help my students discover their realm of origin. These studies have yielded additional information about new realms.

When I first began teaching about the Earth Angel realms, I found that some people couldn't relate to the topic. At first, I assumed that these individuals were "Dabblers," "Shapeshifters," or "Evolvers," meaning that they'd experienced many different realms and couldn't relate to just one.

Eventually, I realized that these folks belonged to new, previously undiscovered realms. As we began to identify them, things began to "click" in my research, so this book is the result of my studies into the new realms. I've also discovered additional information about the realms previously described in *Earth Angels*.

Here, you'll find some of the same material as in the original *Earth Angels* book; however, my prayer and intention is that you'll enjoy the new depth of information that has been discovered since my earlier book was first published.

I believe that there are still some more undiscovered realms that will be found in the years to come, so I welcome your input and letters on the topic.

🌲 🌲 🌲

All of the stories in this book are true, and all of the individuals whose accounts are included here have given written permission for their stories to be published. The names in the book are also real, with the exception of three people who requested pseudonyms, and two who asked that only their initials be used. I'm very grateful to all of them for coming forward and telling their stories, as they enrich all of us by sharing their experiences.

CHAPTER ONE

Are You an Earth Angel?

*D*o you feel different from other people, as if you were dropped off on this planet and wonder when someone's coming to take you home? If so, then you may be an *Earth Angel,* which is another term for *lightworker, Indigo, Crystal,* or one of the other words used to describe a person who incarnated for the express purpose of helping the world be a better place.

Every person is born with a personal mission to learn and grow. Each of us elects a theme for our life in which we'll work on a particular life lesson such as patience, forgiveness, or compassion. Yet Earth Angels also choose a *global* mission in addition to a personal mission . . . and this global mission is to provide a service to the world.

If you have a passion and talent for healing, teaching, or helping others, yet you yourself have substance-abuse problems, weight issues, relationship challenges, and the like, then you may be an Earth Angel. If you're highly sensitive and you abhor violence in any form, then you may very well be an Earth Angel!

Although all souls originate from the same Divine source, our environment and personal history often shape our personalities and physical characteristics. For instance, those who spend most of their time surfing at tropical beaches will have different looks and mannerisms than people who hole up in their inner-city offices every day.

Similarly, all of the lives you've previously lived have impacted you. And, just as your physical family-of-origin influences you, so does your soul's family-of-origin shape your looks, behavior, and even your life purpose.

Again, the *inside* of everyone is the same: a beautiful, pristine spark of Divine light. However, as a lightworker, *your* spark of light may have spent time in heavenly realms far from Earth. Those lifetimes that you've logged in the angelic realm, the elemental kingdom, or on other planets have influenced who you are today. Although you inhabit a human body, your soul feels like a traveler in a foreign country—because that is, in essence, what you are.

Not everyone is an Earth Angel, of course—for this role, God called in the biggest and brightest sparks of light for the transition to the New Age of Peace. Those humans who aren't Earth Angels are living lives purely for their own growth, rest, or enjoyment. They may seem dense or decidedly unspiritual, yet they're Divine sparks of life, too. Their lives have simply been dedicated to human, Earthly concerns.

The Earth Angels' Vital Mission

If you're an Earth Angel, then you're a powerful lightworker with a legacy of healing and miracles behind and in front of you. You accepted your Divine assignment to come to Earth and spread your teachings and healing energies. How has your assignment been so far? If you've had difficulty adjusting to Earthly life, then you'll probably find answers, comfort, and guidance by remembering your spiritual origin.

You may discover that you're an Incarnated Angel or Elemental; a Starperson whose past lives have been extraterrestrial (ET); a Merperson; a Leprechaun; a Knight Paladin; or a Wise One, which is a reincarnated Sorceress, High-Priestess, or Wizard. You're a seasoned service worker called into action—an Earth Angel. You may have had past lives on Earth as an Incarnated Angel, Elemental, and such, yet you forgot these incarnations, believing that your past lives were human.

The term *Earth Angels* is not to be confused with *Incarnated Angels,* which is one of the realms of Earth Angels. By learning about your spiritual realm of origin, you'll understand more about your personality, behavior, and individual quirks. As I mentioned, this is similar to the way our astrological sun signs group us into meaningful categories.

My Early Work with Earth Angels

I first accessed information about Earth Angels through my private practice, where I gave angel, mediumship, and psychic readings. My clients usually consisted of lightworkers who were procrastinating with respect to accomplishing their life mission.

I'll never forget the first Earth Angel I identified during a session. As I scanned her shoulders, looking at her aura and spirit guides, I psychically saw a large artery-like pole extending upward from her left shoulder. As I looked to see where the pole was attached, I gasped. There, spinning above her, was a hovering spacecraft! I had never had any interest in UFOs or ETs and actually found the whole subject intimidating. I hesitated to tell this woman what I saw, but I'd learned to trust my visions and to faithfully deliver them verbatim to my clients. I'd found that even if *I* didn't understand the visions, my clients usually did.

So I inhaled deeply and blurted out, "I see what may be a spacecraft hovering above you."

"Oh, yes," my client replied matter-of-factly. "It's been with me my whole life." This floored me. However, I listened with an open mind as she explained that the ship was her ever-present guide and protector, watching over her and giving her information when needed. She reported having visited the ship during dreamtime sojourns.

Soon after, I saw several other clients with this same extraterrestrial connection. I've always been one to notice personality and behavioral patterns, so I soon noted that my "Starperson clients" had similar aura colors, facial features, relationship patterns, and life missions.

Discovering the Other Realms

Much of the esoteric information that I receive comes from my own guides and angels, who give me messages while I'm sleeping or during readings or meditations. Through these means, I was told of the other soul-group incarnations to look for in my clients and audience members.

First, I studied the *Incarnated Angels*. These men and women have angelic faces, heavyset bodies, histories of codependent relationships, and are perennial helpers. For example, my client Laurie is a quintessential Incarnated Angel. She's a very sweet and attractive blonde nurse with a large, curvy figure and a heart-shaped face. After years of trying to help her alcoholic husband get sober, Laurie finally made the painful decision to divorce him. Now she's searching for a way to transfer her natural healing abilities to a private practice.

I next noticed the group called the *Incarnated Elementals*. My client Jayne is a typical member of this clan. With red hair styled in a pixie cut and a thin, lanky body, Jayne looks like someone who'd wear green elf shoes with curled toes and bell toppings. She's a professional dog groomer and an avid animal-rights advocate who broke off her engagement because her fiancé wanted to move away from the mountains where she grew up.

"He planned to move to the city," Jayne explained. "I'd shrivel up and die if I didn't live near nature—especially if I moved to the city, where trees are practically nonexistent."

For many years, I assumed that these categories were the only realms from which Earth Angels originated: Incarnated Angels,

Elementals, and Starpersons. When I'd discuss these categories with my spiritual counseling students, about 80 percent of them acknowledged an affinity to one of the three groups. I'd even have the students gather into groups with their spiritual clan members. I'd see them crying, laughing together, and exclaiming, "Really? You, too? I'm just like that!" as they swapped stories of Earth life from the perspective of their realm.

But there were always some students who couldn't relate to any of the categories. "What about us humans?" they'd ask.

My son, Grant, finally supplied the answer. He was attending my Angel Therapy Practitioner® certification course in North Miami, giving a brief talk to the class about using candles in rituals and incantations. Grant had been studying Wiccan spirituality for some time, and he had a wealth of knowledge to share. At the end of his talk, he turned to the audience and said, "I know what the fourth category of incarnated lightworkers is. . . . I know, because I'm from this category. It's those of us who are Reincarnated Wizards, High-Priestesses, Witches, Sorcerers, and Sorceresses."

A collective gasp rose from the audience, followed by exclamations of, "Yes! That makes so much sense!" and "That's what I am!" Grant's assessment rang true, and it truly struck a chord with the class participants.

Since then, I've studied and interviewed many people from this group, whom I now call the *Wise Ones*. Whenever I lecture or write about the topic, I receive confirmation that this powerful group of lightworkers relates to this category.

Phyllis typifies the members of this group whom I've met and interviewed. She has an oval face and large eyes, and her faraway stare speaks of someone who sees beyond the physical universe. She wears her hair long; and she has an elegant, almost regal, demeanor. When Phyllis saw the movies *The Mists of Avalon*, *The Lord of the Rings*, and

Harry Potter and the Sorcerer's Stone, she immediately related to the ancient, magical skills that she'd once possessed. Phyllis also knows that she was burned at the stake for being a witch in a prior life.

My original teachings included a fifth category called "Walk-Ins." These are souls who electively take on an adult body so that they can fulfill their life purpose without having to endure childhood and adolescence. While Walk-Ins are highly evolved souls who are serving very important missions, I've realized that they aren't really an Earth Angels' realm of origination. Instead, Walk-Ins are a process. For that reason, they aren't included in this book.

This work includes the new realms that I've found since *Earth Angels* was first published. We now have realms and information for many people who were previously considered "Dabblers," "Shapeshifters," or "Evolvers" (the miscellaneous realm categories). I feel that there are many other yet-undiscovered realms that we'll find eventually, as well. Clearly, this is a field requiring lots of empirical field study.

The Healing Effects of This Knowledge

When I first began publicly discussing this concept, I realized that I was risking being misunderstood, so I limited my discussions to my certification courses because the students who attended were especially open-minded. Even then, I waited until we were deep into our course to talk about Incarnated Angels, Elementals, Wise Ones, and Starpersons.

Each time I discussed the information, the students expressed tremendous relief, and healing followed. Here is how some Earth Angels surveyed for this book described their reactions to discovering their spiritual origin:

- "Since I found out, I've felt relieved. I no longer feel so strange, and I finally have a sense of belonging."

- "Once I leaned about my realm, I realized that nothing was really wrong with the way I acted."

- "It helps me to know that I'm not the only one feeling this way."

- "I've always known that I was different, and now there's an explanation that makes sense."

- "Finally, I realized why I had to help people at all costs. I never knew why I had this drive before."

This healing effect, along with my own guides' urgings and ongoing feeding of information, encouraged me to continue studying this phenomenon.

I had started to write this book several times, yet the moment never seemed quite right—until now—to discuss this topic so openly. I wrote on the subject in one chapter called "Incarnated Angels, Elementals, Walk-Ins, and Starpeople" in my book *Healing with the Angels*. I also wrote an article on the topic, which was reproduced in several metaphysical publications and on my **www.angel therapy.com** Website. The chapter and article attracted a great deal of attention; and at every lecture, audience members requested more details, or asked me to identify their Earth Angel realm.

My former executive assistant, Bronny Daniels, identified herself as a Starperson the first time I delineated the categories. (Like many Starpeople, Bronny is a Reiki master.) She resonated particularly with the Pleiades (a star cluster in the Northern Hemisphere), and told me that she twice had spontaneously channeled the Pleiadeian language. Bronny also strongly suggested that I write this book, and her request finally motivated me to do so, since it finally felt like the right time.

I wrote a proposal for the book, which I submitted to Hay House, my publisher, and

I was told, "We'll talk about it at our upcoming meeting." I started to wonder if this topic might be too weird for them to consider. Bronny and her Starperson friends prayed that Hay House would agree to publish *Earth Angels*. Not only did Hay House say yes, but they also agreed to publish the updated version that you hold in your hands!

Our next step was to survey people who related to the topic of the various Earth Angel incarnations. I first queried my newsletter subscribers, Bronny's Starperson friends, and those who had completed my Angel Therapy Practitioner program. I figured that I would receive a dozen or so completed surveys. Was I ever surprised to discover that the survey was passed around the Internet, and that I received hundreds of responses!

Characteristics of Earth Angels

There are characteristics that apply to all of the Earth Angels, and also those that are unique to each of the realms. The chapters in this book describe each realm's individual distinctions, as well as the common denominators that apply to them—including the following:

— **Feeling different, separate, or alienated from others.** Just about every Earth Angel whom I've met, interviewed, or surveyed has said that they feel "different from others." For all of the realms but the Wise Ones, this characteristic continues into adulthood.

Kelly, who is an Incarnated Angel, describes the feeling in this way: "I feel like I don't fit in. I always felt that I was a social outcast. When I was in grade school, the other children always told me I was weird. I used to take it extremely personally, and think, *Nobody likes me.* I would sit and cry for hours. I felt so helpless and sorry for myself because I didn't know why they perceived me as being different.

"I was determined to fit in, and I wanted so badly for everyone to love me. But the only thing that really helped me feel like I belonged was to do things for other people. Later, I became aware of how many people were taking advantage of my niceness.

"Now that I understand my origin as an Incarnated Angel, I'm able to look at situations with a different perspective. It's okay to be different. It's okay to be me. This is how I'm supposed to be. Now I don't have to do things for people to make them like me."

Many Earth Angels have been teased or verbally abused because of their different appearance, interests, and behavior. As Terry, a Starperson, recalled, "My sisters always introduced me as 'the one who was dropped off by a UFO.'" Now Terry realizes the kernel of truth in her sisters' taunts, and their words no longer sting her.

— **Intense sensitivity to other people, chemicals, or violence in any form.** Earth Angels have difficulty being in crowds, feeling bombarded by the overwhelming emotions and physical sensations emanating from other people. Most Earth Angels have learned to avoid harsh chemicals in their food, cleaning supplies, and toiletries due to allergic reactions. Violence in any form repels Earth Angels, including arguments, negative media reports, and violent movies. People often tease them for this trait, saying, "You're just too sensitive!" Yet, this sensitivity is a sacred gift that Earth Angels bring to this planet, enabling them to intuitively know where their services are needed. They couldn't turn off their sensitivity if they tried!

Earth Angel Shelly says, "I've always disliked being in crowds, and in places where there's noise and chaos. Quite often, my level of empathy is more of a problem than a blessing. I often feel scattered and disoriented at the slightest raise in energy. I have difficulty living with other people, so I do best when I live alone."

— **A strong sense of purpose.** Even if the Earth Angel doesn't specifically know what his or her purpose is, there's a sense that the mission involves teaching and healing others. As an Incarnated Angel named Stav put it, "I've always known that my life's mission was to teach, heal, and serve, and to do my part in helping out our troubled world. Although I'm not sure what I signed up for, I'm willing to help."

— **A history of frustrating relationship patterns.** Earth Angels are often raised by emotionally unavailable or abusive parents. As adults, they may attract abusive friends and lovers. Many Earth Angels have love relationships with partners who are unfaithful, physically or verbally abusive, or noncommittal. Some Earth Angels are "sent" to dysfunctional families as children to act as healing catalysts.

These young Earth Angels feel like adoptees, since they don't relate to their parents or siblings at all. And truly, these are their *physical* families and not their spiritual families. Other Earth Angels sign up for challenging family situations so that they can progress extra fast during one lifetime. Only a strong commitment to understanding and healing this pattern seems to break the spell cast over their subsequent relationships.

— **Strangers telling them their problems, as well as really personal information.** Earth Angels have lifelong histories of being approached by total strangers who ask for help or divulge intimate details about their lives. People often tell Earth Angels, "There's just something about you that I can trust."

Alisann says, "This has happened to me all my life. I can be standing in a room full of people, and someone will come over and tell me their most intimate information, without my asking them to." This tendency is especially true among Incarnated Angels, as members of the other realms have learned how they can use their body language to discourage this practice.

— **Looking younger than their chronological years.** Perhaps it's because they eat more healthfully, exercise, and take care of themselves better overall—or maybe it's their spiritual outlook—but Earth Angels often appear younger than their chronological age. Nearly every Earth Angel surveyed reported that people are shocked when they discover their true age. One Earth Angel said that she was carded for buying alcohol until she was well into her 30s. The exception is Wise Ones, whose hair often grays prematurely and whose somber facial expressions can look more mature than their chronological age.

— **Possibly having a history of personal and familial addictions.** Whether food, drugs, alcohol, cigarettes, relationships, or all of the above, some Earth Angels turn to outside substances or influences to numb the pain of feeling different and of being intimidated by their life's mission. One Earth Angel described it in this way: "I found it much easier to cope with life when I used drugs and alcohol. These substances brought me a lightness, or a feeling of numbness, to allow me to forget why I was here. The drugs would put my mission on the back burner. It was more of a worthiness issue back then."

— **A ringing sound in one ear.** Most Earth Angels (although not all) notice a high-pitched ringing sound in one ear. The sound may accompany stressful situations or come out of the blue. Many Earth Angels consider this an annoying distraction, but the ringing is actually encoded information downloaded from the Earth Angels' realm to help them rise above Earthly problems. It also includes instructions and guidance for the Earth Angels' mission. Fortunately, Earth

Angels can mentally ask heaven to reduce the volume or pitch of the sound so that it no longer hurts their ears.

🌿　🌿　🌿

This is a book for and about *you!* My prayer is that it will help you heal wounds you may have suffered as a result of feeling different, being highly sensitive, extremely creative, or fitting outside the parameters of norms, expectations, and organizations.

🌿　🌿　🌿

How to Know What Realm You're From

Each chapter describes one or more of the known Earth Angel realms. Read each chapter to uncover which realm you may originate from. Pay attention to your body's signals such as chill bumps, muscular responses, or a sense of déjà vu. If you find yourself relating to more than one realm (or none of them), you may be from an as-yet-undiscovered realm or from a blend of two or more realms.

Each realm has unique eye characteristics, so this is one way to distinguish someone's realm origination. You can also ask your open-minded friends to help you determine your realm. In addition, graduates of my Angel Therapy Practitioner and Angel Intuitive® programs can give you educated guidance about the realms. Some of them even teach workshops on the topic.

No matter what realm you're from, you're a beloved child of the Creator. You, like everyone, have an important life purpose, and I'm very glad that you elected to incarnate on Earth at this time!

⋙ ✳ ⋘

CHAPTER TWO

Incarnated Angels

*R*eports of Incarnated Angels date back at least to the time of Apostle Paul, who wrote to the Hebrews: "Do not forget to entertain strangers, for by so doing some have unwittingly entertained angels." My books *Angel Visions*, *Angel Visions II,* and *My Guardian Angel* (Hay House, 2007) include stories of people who have encountered humans who are Incarnated Angels.

Some angels briefly take on human form to prevent a tragedy, and then vanish without a trace before the humans involved have a chance to say thank you. Yet, there are other Incarnated Angels who elect to live their entire lives in a human body—and they're probably among the dearest lightworkers imaginable.

> *When you look into the eyes of an Incarnated Angel, you see sweet, pure, unconditional love.*

Incarnated Angels tend to:

- Have sweet, heart-shaped faces

- Apologize and say "I'm sorry" frequently

- "Look" like angels (whether male or female)

- Have cupid-bow lips and large doe-like eyes that radiate innocence and love

- Have overeating or weight issues

- Be professional helpers, such as teachers, flight attendants, nurses, and counselors

- Lighten or highlight their hair (no matter what their genetic race is)

- Be very trusting of people

- Have difficulty saying no and feel guilty when others help them

- Love angels; and have collections of angel statues, books, jewelry, etc.

- Have extra guardian angels

- Seem to glow, with a huge aura around them

- Fall in love with someone's potential and try to coach that person to greatness

- Have codependent relationships with addicts and alcoholics

- Stay in relationships much longer than the average person would

As mentioned in Chapter 1, each realm has unique eye characteristics. The Incarnated Angels have pure, sweet innocence in their eyes. They radiate unconditional love, much like a baby deer's eyes.

I'm often asked about *Reincarnated Angels*. The term *Incarnated* is more accurate, though, than *Reincarnated*. An angel may have lived more than one life in human form, but if its most recent lifetime was angelic, the telltale characteristics belie their true spiritual origins.

Many Incarnated Angels struggle with health challenges, especially fibromyalgia, chronic fatigue syndrome, and gynecological problems. Louise L. Hay, the author of *Heal Your Body* (Hay House), says that female health issues stem from "denial of the self and rejecting femininity"; and that fibroid tumors and cysts come from "nursing a hurt from a partner, and a blow to the feminine ego."

These symptoms could apply equally well to male and female Incarnated Angels, who look past the surface when they meet people and see their inner talents, divinity, and potential. Incarnated Angels share these characteristics with angels in the spirit world, who only focus upon inner beauty, and urge humans to polish their natural talents in order to make the world a better place.

Incarnated Angels often have friends and lovers who mask their potential with addictions. Incarnated Angels take on these relationships as an "assignment," trying to help others overcome their self-doubts and focus upon their strengths and talents. Unfortunately, this often leads to frustrating relationships for both parties. Incarnated Angels feel thwarted by trying to heal and fix their partners. And the partners wonder, "Why are you trying to change me?" Many Incarnated Angels fantasize that if they did enough for their partners, or gave them enough love, these people would finally heal. This is fine as long as these individuals believe that a need to heal exists—and are *ready* to heal.

My experience with clients who suffer from gynecological problems, breast issues, and prostate issues is that they also suffer from the "women and men who love too much" syndrome. There's really no such thing as giving too much love. However, when a person gives love and *then resents* the fact that it's not appreciated or reciprocated, the stuffed anger can manifest in physical symptoms.

Many Incarnated Angels have histories of abusive relationships, so if they hold on to toxic emotions related to this abuse, their bodies naturally protest.

Energy, Weight, and Food

A propensity toward chronic fatigue syndrome also provides other clues about the nature of Incarnated Angels, as all of the Earth Angel realms are extremely sensitive to energy. Yet, Incarnated Angels may be especially vulnerable to toxic energies and energy drains because of their "women and men who love too much" predilection. Incarnated Angels are much more people oriented and more likely to work in a large corporation, compared to the other types of Earth Angels.

Incarnated Angels need to practice energy shielding and clearing techniques, as described in the next section. Otherwise, it's like going out into a blizzard without a jacket. An Incarnated Angel named Kelly says that this practice helped her enormously. She explains, "Whenever a particular co-worker would walk by or stop to talk to me, I would feel absolutely drained. I could swear that he was snatching my energy. Soon afterward, I read about some people having 'hooks' in their energy field, where their energy reaches out and takes your own energy from you. After observing that this was occurring, I used the exercises in the book to protect my energy. Shortly thereafter, this man stopped coming around me."

Taking good care of their energy also helps Incarnated Angels avoid using food to boost their vitality. Many Incarnated Angels are compulsive overeaters, and it's very common for these lightworkers to carry extra weight on their bodies. Yasmin, an Incarnated Angel, says, "Being a chocoholic provides me with daily, exquisite reminders of heaven; and it's very hard for me to go without chocolate as a result."

Food provides a way for Incarnated Angels to ground themselves when they feel spaced-out; and it's also an outlet for stress, especially crunchy, salty foods such as potato chips and popcorn.

It seems that the reason so many Inca
Angels are overweight is not due to over
ing, but because they're energetically shieldii
themselves with fat. They have difficulty losing
weight, even with stringent dieting or exercise.
This is especially true among Incarnated Angels
who are massage therapists, or who are otherwise engaged in healing touch. They absorb
their clients' toxic emotions, and their bodies
blow up like sponges absorbing water.

With their voluptuous bodies, exquisitely
beautiful faces, and large hairdos, female
Incarnated Angels look like plus-size beauty
queens. They're often told, "You have such a
pretty face. If only you'd lose weight, you'd
be gorgeous!" Actresses Delta Burke and Elizabeth Taylor are examples of Incarnated Angels
with these physical characteristics.

Male Incarnated Angels are burly teddy-
bear types, such as actor John Goodman; or
those with sweet and boyish faces, such as
actor John Dye (Andrew on the TV program
Touched by an Angel).

utside into the rain, you

Well, in a similar fashion,

necessary to put on your "energy jacket" each time you engage in helping another person. When you open your heart toward another, you're also open to receiving residual fear-energy they may spew in your direction. That doesn't mean you shouldn't help, but it's just like helping those who have been out in the rain for a while: They may have a lot of mud on them, and it doesn't help anybody if that mud transfers to you. In other words, when you help others clean up their thoughts and emotions, they release the toxins, which may splatter on whoever's near—including you, the helper.

Those of you who are Incarnated Angels tend to be the "bleeding hearts" of the Earth Angel realms, and you particularly need to remember to use shielding techniques prior to conducting any healing work. Otherwise, you're liable to put on extra body fat to protect and insulate yourself. The extra fat doesn't necessarily come from overeating, and you'll find that the weight doesn't budge in response to dieting and exercise. However, the padding is a form of protection that you can swap for a layer of protective energy, or *shielding.*

It only takes a moment to energetically shield yourself. Ideally, you would do this before *any* helping/healing session—whether it's a paid or volunteer session is irrelevant. It also doesn't matter whether the person you're helping is a stranger, a client, a family member, or a friend. And it doesn't matter how long the helping session lasts—it could be a brief moment or several days. Whenever you're about to help someone, shield yourself.

Still, if you forget to shield yourself *before* the session, you can still shield yourself any time *during* the session. It's never too late to shield yourself; however, by then you may have absorbed some psychic debris, so you'll want to engage in *clearing* afterward. (The next section describes this process.)

Just by holding the intention to shield yourself with a protective layer of light and energy makes it happen. It's done. You really can't do it wrong, or be denied access to the light or energy shield. Anyone who holds this intention receives immediate results, without exception.

Shielding means visualizing, feeling, and/or thinking of yourself surrounded in a cocoon of light. This light is the essence of angels; and it's a living, loving, intelligent entity that you've called to surround and protect you. Don't worry. This light is always of the Divine Light of our Creator. So-called dark forces don't have this light available to share with others (nor would they want to do so even if they could). So, you can't accidentally call in a lower energy when you shield yourself.

You can shield yourself in various colors of light, depending upon your intention.

Again, know that your intention to surround yourself with this light won't be denied. Anyone who asks will receive, without exception (although the ego sometimes tries to convince us otherwise, and please don't listen to that voice!). The different colors include the following:

— **White light:** This invokes the angels around you to surround you without interruption. The angels protect you, and they ensure that you're safe and guarded.

— **Pink light:** This is the light to invoke if you're with a negative person who's obsessed with their problems. The pink light sends loving energy outward toward everyone who talks with you, and simultaneously sends loving energy inward toward yourself.

Nothing can permeate this pink shield except loving thoughts and energies.

— **Emerald green light:** See or feel yourself surrounded by this light whenever you want to heal some imbalance in your physical body. Your body absorbs this light wherever it needs healing energy.

— **Purple light:** Imagine yourself shrouded in royal purple light, which elevates your spiritual frequency, enabling you to rise above problems and contact the highest level of Divine guidance. Purple light also bounces away any lower energies, entities, or earthbound spirits.

— **Rainbow light:** See or feel yourself wearing a coat of rainbow stripes, which boosts your ability to conduct energy healing work on yourself or others.

You can shield yourself in layers of multi-colored light if you choose, in order to invoke all of the beneficial effects of the various colors. For instance, you can visualize a triple layer of light, with white light first for angelic energy, followed by a layer of emerald green light for healing, and then purple light to elevate your consciousness to the highest truth.

You can also use shielding to protect your loved ones, your home, your vehicles, your city or country, and the world. Just use the same methods in order to envision those people, objects, places, or areas surrounded by healing light.

Clearing

It's possible that you'll forget to shield yourself before a session, so you'll want to regularly engage in energy clearing in order to wash away the effects of fear from your own thoughts, or from the thoughts of others. Fatigue is the main symptom of absorbing these lower energies. This type of fatigue doesn't respond to caffeine, naps, or exercise. The sensation of profound tiredness is chronic, because it's coming from sources foreign to your physical body. Don't worry, though . . . you can easily remove the cause, as well as its effect of fatigue.

After each healing or teaching session, or whenever you feel very tired, use energy-clearing techniques. Your own guides and angels may teach you methods that uniquely suit you, but here are some of my favorites:

— **Cutting your cords:** This is an essential step for all healers and teachers. Each of your students and clients attach etheric cords to you when they believe that they need something from you. Then, after your session, they draw energy from you. They may also send toxic energy through the cords *toward* you. This is a mostly unconscious process, although the cords are visible clairvoyantly, and palpable clairsentiently.

To cut the cords, simply say this aloud or mentally:

> *"Archangel Michael, please come to me now and cut the cords of fear that are draining my energy and vitality."*

If you're truly ready to release these cords, Archangel Michael will instantly fulfill your request. Sometimes people hang on to cords because of an unhealthy "need to be needed." If this is the case, ask Archangel Michael to help you release the fears behind such a desire. (Remember that the archangels can be with everyone who calls on them simultaneously, and that they don't have time or space restrictions.)

— **Taking sea-salt baths:** If there's no ocean nearby to swim in, you can mimic its healing effects by filling your bathtub with warm water and sea salts, which are available at any health-food store or spa. The pure salt draws out toxic energies from your pores. Be sure to choose a brand without artificial colors or synthetic scents so that you don't inadvertently introduce more chemicals into your body.

— **Connecting with nature:** Plants and animals provide a welcome respite from artificial lighting, electromagnetic frequencies, ringing telephones, and pressures from other people. Plants also draw negative toxins out of our mental, emotional, and physical bodies. When you feel tired, take a walk outdoors. Also, keep a potted plant next to your bed so that the plant and its fairies can conduct energy clearing work on you while you sleep.

Angels and Assertiveness

Incarnated Angels are born to help and heal, and they come to Earth ready to enact this mission. However, this eagerness can create difficulties if it's unbalanced.

For example, Incarnated Angels carry such optimism about (and love for) humanity that they often have difficulty saying no. Assertiveness training from a counselor, class, or self-help book or tape may be necessary, since many Incarnated Angels say no to themselves in the form of self-denial, while saying yes to everyone else.

Incarnated Angels often apologize for asking for help, or don't delegate at all, and then resent the fact that no one's helping them and that they have to do all of the work. This can result in a "martyr/victim complex" in which the Incarnated Angels feel like everyone is taking advantage of them instead of realizing they've created the situation. Some Incarnated Angels feel guilty asking for help, even when asking their own guardian angels for assistance, due to a fear of "bothering" them. Sometimes this fear stems from years of being teased or verbally abused. The Incarnated Angels believe that there's something wrong with them, so they don't believe that they deserve assistance. They may develop a pattern of self-sabotage and push away opportunities.

The way to heal in this area is to reframe the whole topic of "receiving." This means that these angels need to realize that they can give and help others more if they allow themselves to first receive. For example, if they feel compelled to be healers, they may need a healing center, money for advertising, a computer, or other accoutrements. They may also need extra money to quit a job that takes their time away from their healing practice.

Related to this is that some Earth Angels, including Incarnated Angels, have difficulty accepting money for their healing treatments. This can create a problem in the case of Incarnated Angels who want to quit meaningless jobs on which they're financially dependent. If they'd accept money for spiritual healing or counseling, they could afford to quit their jobs and become full-time healers or teachers.

It's important for client and healer to exchange energy during healing and teaching sessions. In other words, the client or student needs to give something back. This could be money, food, services, or a donation to the healer or teacher's favorite charity. Encouraging a client or student to give back is part of the healing process offered by an Incarnated Angel.

Many Incarnated Angels have "giving and receiving imbalances." The Law of Giving and Receiving means that whenever we give, we automatically receive. It's the flow and the core of the Universe. And clearly,

Incarnated Angels spend much of their time giving. In fact, most of them work in helping professions, such as medicine, teaching, counseling, or the travel industry. However, they often block the flow of receiving for themselves through self-sabotage, self-denial, and wasteful spending.

Female energy is receptive energy, and when a female Incarnated Angel gives too much, she can become unbalanced with too much masculine energy. This is also true for male Incarnated Angels. Giving continually, without taking time out for themselves, is another reason why Incarnated Angels may suffer from fatigue.

The affirmations to heal this imbalance are: "I receive good graciously," and "The more that I allow myself to receive, the better able I am to help others." If Incarnated Angels would affirm these words repeatedly and adopt the habit of self-pampering, they'd be more open to receiving in other ways, such as accepting help with their mission. Healthy

Incarnated Angels realize that they accelerate God's plan of peace if they work as a team, asking and receiving help from each other.

Incarnated Angels feel very comfortable following rules, and they may be afraid of breaking them. They are hard workers, often bordering on perfectionism in their careers. In fact, the surveys submitted for this book by Incarnated Angels were painstakingly neat and well organized, in comparison to surveys submitted by the other realms. These characteristics make it comfortable for them to work in institutional or academic settings. Many Incarnated Angels work for hospitals, school systems, and airlines. Female Incarnated Angels are frequently employed as nurses, teachers, and flight attendants, or any job requiring a loving heart and saintly patience. I've always thought that it was particularly fitting that so many flight attendants are Incarnated Angels, because after all, angels are accustomed to flying!

The Personal Lives of Incarnated Angels

Because Incarnated Angels are physically attractive and have big, loving hearts, they rarely have difficulty attracting romantic partners or friends. Their difficulty is in finding *fulfilling* relationships, however. Incarnated Angels often see their romantic partners and their friends as potential clients whom they can help and teach. They approach new relationships with the question: "How can I help this person?"

As mentioned earlier, Incarnated Angels often fall in love with addicts and then try to fix them. In friendships, they often play the role of counselor. For instance, Incarnated Angels may find themselves listening to their friends' problems for hours. When they try to talk about their own issues, the friends suddenly end the conversation. This is another instance in which the Incarnated Angels' lives are unbalanced as far as giving and receiving. Who listens to *their* troubles?

As mentioned earlier, Incarnated Angels may have been "sent" into dysfunctional families as their guardian angels, so they may feel entirely disconnected from their birth families and even wonder if they were adopted, as they have nothing in common. These people don't feel like "family" to the Incarnated Angels, and in truth, they aren't. The family members are stranger-souls whom the Incarnated Angels volunteered to help by coming into human bodies and living with them.

With their tendency to see the goodness and potential in others, Incarnated Angels often remain in unhealthy relationships. They stay put well past the time when the average person would have left.

Pamela, an Incarnated Angel, describes her love relationship pattern in this way: "I attract men who have wounded hearts and are really in need of healing. I remain optimistic that they'll heal and that my love will transform them, but that doesn't happen. I have a very hard time ending these relationships, and it takes me a long time to process the pain and separation."

Incarnated Angels often commit to relationships quickly; and soon after the first date they may decide to "go steady," get married or engaged, or live with the new partner. Incarnated Angel Elizabeth says, "I always start to get serious with men right away, although there are things that I don't like about them. I have trouble just dating."

Since Incarnated Angels leap before they look in marriage, and also marry for the first time when they're very young, they may develop a history of multiple marriages or marriagelike relationships. Many Incarnated Angels surveyed for this book were on their third or fourth marriage. They had a new husband or wife every ten years or so. Again, think of Elizabeth Taylor as a quintessential example.

Many Incarnated Angels have difficulty ending unhealthy relationships with lovers, friends, or abusive family members. Like compulsive gamblers, they think that if they keep trying, eventually the relationship will pay off. Incarnated Angels live by the Golden Rule and don't want to abandon others—since they have a great fear of being abandoned themselves. They're also reluctant to be honest about their needs and feelings. So, Incarnated Angels suffer silently in a relationship, taking out their unhappiness on themselves. Eventually, they reach the point of not being able to take it anymore. That's when the Incarnated Angel either leaves or pushes the other person away.

Incarnated Angels may have unbalanced and unhealthy friendships and love relationships, too. Friendships are based upon give-and-take, but these types of relationships are usually one-sided, with the Incarnated Angels always being the helpers and never the "helpees." The Incarnated Angels are supposed to be the strong ones in any relationship; and the "friends" are entitled to unlimited free-of-charge counseling, healing sessions, and psychic readings.

Eventually, Incarnated Angels burn out from this type of lopsided "friendship." They realize that their "friends" have no interest in them, except in how the Incarnated Angels can help them. The Incarnated Angels may feel trapped in a mire of guilt, though, as if they're abandoning friends in need. The "law of attraction" also causes them to lose interest in friends who don't share their beliefs.

It helps if Incarnated Angels have support, especially from other angels who understand. The 12-step groups Al-Anon and Co-Dependents Anonymous both provide wonderful support for Incarnated Angels trying to heal their relationships. Study groups for *A Course in Miracles* are also powerful places to heal from guilt. Incarnated Angels can probably be found at any event or place involving angels, such as angel seminars, angel shops, or book-study groups that are studying texts about these heavenly beings.

Every relationship is an "assignment," with the potential for both partners to learn and grow. No one is a victim in relationships—they're all chosen, either consciously or on a soul level.

Incarnated Angel Nicole says, "I've been in four marriage-like relationships. All of them have been with men who were emotionally unavailable and abusers, cheaters, and drug addicts. Although my friends and family thought I was a victim, I knew that they could never see what I could in the souls of these men. I knew that on some level, I was helping to raise their vibration.

"My last relationship was the most difficult and painful. One day I was looking out the window and I told God that I could no longer stay in this relationship. In that moment, I heard the angels say to me, 'We know it is painful; please stay a little longer.' I felt completely loved, and had the strength to finish my work with this man. I'm now with a kind man who's my soul mate and who's on his spiritual path. He knows that I'm an Earth Angel, and he loves me just the way I am."

Spread Your Wings and Fly!

An Incarnated Angel's eyes are filled with wide-eyed compassion and love. The reflection of some personal pain is evident, but it's outweighed by the look of Divine Love. Incarnated Angels look past the surface and see the potential within each person. In contrast, an Incarnated Elemental's eyes reflect pure, playful mischief; and a Wise One's eyes have the haunting and faraway look of hard-won lessons.

Incarnated Angels have the classic physical features of angels that artists have captured. They look like angels, whether male or female. With their sweet faces and dispositions, people will call them "angel" without realizing the profound truth of that statement. As Pamela says, "Many people have come up to me and said, 'You look just like an angel,' or 'You're so angelic.' Often these are those who aren't familiar with my work or my love for angels." Many people report clairvoyantly seeing large feathered wings extending from the shoulder blades of Incarnated Angels, and a glowing white light emanating from their bodies.

Like the other Earth Angel realms, it's important for Incarnated Angels to let their lights shine, even if they're afraid of ridicule or rejection. One Incarnated Angel said, "There's a part of me that wants to fold my angel wings and hide my true identity sometimes. This manifests as sometimes not doing my healing work or missing deadlines for advertising my practice."

Yet, when Incarnated Angels spread their wings and fly, it's sheer beauty to behold. Incarnated Angel Judi has realized the importance of surrendering all of her fears to her guardian angels: "At this time, I know that I'm definitely on the right path. All of the desires of my heart are being manifested before me now that I've surrendered and released my life to the service of the angels. Nothing can ever take that away from me. My life purpose and my path have never been clearer or more rewarding. I struggled for so many years, and now I feel like I'm floating on a cloud most of the time!"

Life-Path Work for Incarnated Angels

Incarnated Angels are often attracted to the helping professions, and they make wonderful healers and counselors (traditional or nontraditional); schoolteachers; and members of the travel industry. Most Incarnated Angels enjoy one-on-one work more than working with groups or speaking in front of groups. They're very adept at working in large companies, provided that management has a humanitarian work ethic. Incarnated Angels are miserable working for unethical bosses or firms.

Guidance and Suggestions
If You're an Incarnated Angel

If you're an Incarnated Angel, you'll have a more peaceful and prosperous time on Earth if you remember to do the following:

— **Shield yourself with energy and light, especially before helping someone.** This will reduce your need to overeat in order to protect yourself with a layer of extra body weight.

— **Wait before saying yes.** Instead of automatically agreeing to every request for help, give yourself time to meditate, and think about whether it's something that truly is part of your mission and your heart's desire. When people ask something of you, tell them, "Let me think about it," or "I'll get back to you on this." These individuals will respect the fact that you're taking care of yourself.

— **Replace the apology habit with positive affirmations.** Incarnated Angels habitually apologize when they've done nothing wrong. This habit stems from the desire to keep everyone happy, even if it means shifting the blame to themselves.

To boost the happiness quotient of yourself and other people, use positive words instead. Adopt the habit of speaking about yourself, others, and situations with uplifting phrases.

— **Engage in cardiovascular exercise.** This helps in stress and weight management and is important for Incarnated Angels' healthy hearts.

— **Balance your giving and receiving quotas.** Be sure to give *yourself* treats regularly.

— **Drop any rules that restrict your mission.** Notice whether you have personal "rules" you follow without question, such as, "I better not get too successful, or people will be jealous of me and feel pain from this jealousy." Question rules by asking, "Is this rule working *for* my mission or against it?"

— **Delegate.** Ask for help without apologizing.

— **Accept good graciously.** Allow people to give you assistance, presents, and compliments.

— **Play.** Allow your inner child plenty of time to be silly, free, and creative.

≽ ✳ ≼

CHAPTER THREE

Incarnated Elementals

*T*his is one of the easiest groups to recognize among the realms. Like the Incarnated Angels, Incarnated Elementals physically look like their namesakes—that is, fairies, elves, pixies, gnomes, incarnated animals, and unicorns. Besides the guardian angels that we all have, this group has fairies as their protective spirits.

Very often, members of this group have reddish hair (whether it is full-on red, auburn, or strawberry blonde); and a Celtic heritage or appearance, such as a ruddy complexion or freckles.

Angel or Elemental?

Perhaps you saw yourself in the previous chapter about Incarnated Angels. Still, you identify strongly with the descriptions of Elementals. If you're confused about whether you're an Incarnated Angel or an Elemental, here are four questions you can ask yourself to help you distinguish between the two realms:

1. **How do I feel about rules?** If you're an Incarnated Angel, you usually obey rules and get angry at people who break them. However, if you're an Incarnated Elemental, then you can't stand rules and think that people who abide by them are wimps.

2. **Is there mischief in my eyes?** Elementals are fun-loving beings, often practical jokers, and are always looking for a laugh. Incarnated Angels

tend to be serious and polite. If you wonder whether you're an Angel or an Elemental, ask a close friend if you have here-comes-trouble eyes. This is a characteristic unique to Elementals. (If you vacillate between being "naughty" and "nice," then you may be a MerAngel, which is a hybrid blend of the Angel and Elemental realms discussed in Chapter 6.)

When you look into the eyes of an Incarnated Elemental, you see twinkles of mischief or playfulness.

3. **What type of wings do I have?**
    Angels have feathered wings, while many Elementals have butterfly or dragonfly wings. The wings are etheric, not physical.

To determine your wing type, either consult a clairvoyant, or go within and feel for yourself. Focus upon your shoulder blades and feel or see (in your mind's eye) whether the wings are large, feathery, swan-like appendages, or more like buzzing and beautiful butterfly or dragonfly wings.

Also, note your body type: Incarnated Elementals usually have slim bodies, fast metabolisms, and sensitive nervous systems; while Incarnated Angels have voluptuous bodies, slow metabolisms, and mellow personalities. The exceptions are Merpeople, who are voluptuous hybrids of both the Angel and Elemental realms, which is discussed in Chapter 6.

4. **What is my relationship to addictions?** Most Incarnated Angels are codependents, while Elementals

are the addicts. Elementals love to party; Angels love to rescue! The exception is that many Incarnated Angels are addicted to food.

5. **What is my disposition?** Elementals tend to have fiery, passionate personality styles, while Incarnated Angels are patient and calm (or at least appear that way to others).

Other Distinguishing Characteristics

Sometimes Incarnated Elementals are unsure whether they might actually be from the realm of the Wise Ones. That's because Elementals have ancient histories and relationships with wizards, witches, and sorceresses. So the Wise Ones feel very familiar to Incarnated Elementals. After all, the Elementals were present when the witches were burned, so they may have residual pain from that era, even though they themselves weren't killed. They may have memories of the burnings and confuse them with their own recollections. The primary difference is that Elementals are much more playful than Wise Ones, who tend to be extremely serious, or even somber or stern.

In fact, Incarnated Elementals sometimes get themselves into trouble with their wacky sense of humor. Their jokes may be ill timed, offensive, off-color, or just plain inappropriate. But one of the Incarnated Elementals' missions is to get the world to lighten up, smile, and laugh—even at their own expense.

In the spiritual Elemental kingdom, the fairies, elves, and others hold nightly parties filled with dancing, singing, storytelling, and laughter. They know the spiritual value of playfulness and joy! Not surprisingly, their human counterparts also know how to enjoy themselves. Incarnated Elementals often become professional entertainers, including comedians, actors, dancers, and musicians. Some examples are comedians Carol Burnett, Ellen DeGeneres, Eddie Murphy, Robin Williams, and Red Skelton; actress Julia Roberts; and socialite Paris Hilton.

Relationship Issues for Incarnated Elementals

The Elementals were tired of humans' assault on nature, animals, and the environment. They couldn't make headway as tiny spiritual beings, so they elected to take on human lives and bodies to have more power and say-so in cleaning Earth's air, water, and soil; and in helping the animals.

Truth be told, Elementals prefer the company of animals or plants to people. They feel an innate anger toward the human race for hurting the planet. Spiritual Elementals are said to be vicious pranksters, but they're only mischievous toward humans who show disrespect for the environment. On the other hand, they love to help humans who recycle, use Earth-friendly cleaning products, treat animals kindly, and respect Mother Nature. Some of the Elementals' practical jokes are passive-aggressive, stemming from their lack of respect for humans' wasteful ways.

In relationships, romantic partners are attracted to Incarnated Elementals because of their comedic, musical, or artistic skills. But after the relationship begins, Incarnated Elementals may be accused of being "bratty," "immature," "noncommittal," or "stubborn." They exhibit the same personality traits as tiny elves, fairies, gnomes, and the like. In the spiritual Elemental kingdom, these beings are often flirtatious and promiscuous. Incarnated Elementals may exhibit these characteristics in their relationships as well.

The Elementals are much less people oriented than Incarnated Angels. They like to associate with others so they can party, but then they want to be left alone afterward.

Elementals are also prone to substance abuse and addictions. So, in essence, while Incarnated Angels marry addicts, Incarnated Elementals *are* the addicts.

Many Incarnated Elementals are in helping professions involving people, but usually because they have a "calling" to do so. Like the Hobbit Frodo in the book and movie *The Lord of the Rings*, Incarnated Elementals are reluctant heroes who help people because they *have to,* not necessarily because they *want to.*

They need a lot of space and alone time, especially outside in nature. Elementals can be shy and very private, even though they're extroverted in social gatherings. They appear to be very open about their private lives, yet there's a guardedness that keeps them from revealing their deepest secrets unless they absolutely trust a person—and that's very rare. They may have an "off-with-their-heads" policy about people in their lives. In other words, when Incarnated Elementals are done with a relationship, they're *really* done.

Incarnated Elementals have learned how to signal people when they don't want to be bothered. Evie speaks for many Elementals when she says, "Strangers used to come up to me and tell me their troubles, but I closed off a bit over the years because I had such a problem taking on other people's stuff."

Incarnated Elementals are clowns when they feel comfortable, especially when surrounded by other fun-loving Incarnated Elementals. In dysfunctional families, they may play the role of "mascot," helping the family cheer up and feel better about themselves. Yet, Incarnated Elementals are also sensitive to disapproval; and so may become introverted, shy, or even reclusive at times when they don't feel socially "safe." They often turn to drugs or alcohol to feel comfortable in social situations.

Compared to other Earth Angel realms, Incarnated Elementals are a physically robust group, reporting very few health problems, perhaps because Elementals are more apt to spend time outdoors, hiking and exercising in fresh air and sunshine. Or, maybe the Elementals' optimism makes them minimize or deny health concerns. The only noticeable health pattern in the surveys submitted by Incarnated Elementals was a high frequency of depression, and several Incarnated Elementals said they had histories of childhood asthma. This corresponds with reports that fairies are sensitive to airborne chemicals and need to avoid pesticides in their gardens and foods. It could also be claustrophobia from spending too much time indoors, since the Elemental soul needs healthy doses of fresh air.

Manifestation and Magic

The spiritual Elementals know how to manifest all of their needs. This is one reason why they approach their tasks, like tending to flowers, with playful joy. The Elementals know that hard work isn't a necessity in order to create meaningful results—intention and sincerity are more important.

Incarnated Elementals often eschew hard work, and may be perceived as slackers who favor socializing instead of working. They unconsciously recall lifetimes in the spiritual Elemental kingdom where they could manifest material needs (food, clothing, gold, housing, and so on) out of thin air.

As a result, many Incarnated Elementals feel off center in the workaday world of human beings, and they begin to manifest poverty for themselves. The Incarnated Elementals whom I've met seem to either create feast or famine. I rarely meet Incarnated Elementals who have achieved financial security unless they're consciously working a process of manifestation, such as the one outlined in John Randolph Price's *The Abundance Book* (Hay House). Then the magic begins! Elementals—like the Wise Ones' realm—have magical manifestation abilities. When harnessed, these abilities can bend time and physical laws, and create rapid manifestations and miracles.

Incarnated Elementals have fairies, elves, or leprechauns with them as spirit guides; and they can call upon these benevolent helpers at any time by thinking the thought, *Please help me!*

Elementals and Nature

Incarnated Elementals are truly people of the earth and her spirit. They have great difficulty being indoors for long. While Incarnated Angels are comfortable working in large windowless buildings, it would be devastating to an Incarnated Elemental. They *must* be outside in nature or they become depressed. The happiest Elementals are those who create outdoor jobs, such as leading nature hikes or retreats, working at plant nurseries, working as forest rangers, gardening, or dog walking, for example.

If Incarnated Elementals must work indoors, they should request the office with a window facing a park or grassy area. Similarly, Elementals are happiest with offices that are crammed with potted trees, plants, crystals, and flowers. Playing recordings of nature sounds, such as singing birds, the ocean surf, rain, and the like is also beneficial. In addition, their offices should sport photos of their favorite pets, and statues of fairies and elves. Aromatherapy with genuine (not synthetic) essential oils of plants and flowers helps Elementals stay connected to Mother Earth when they're indoors. (These oils are available at most health-food stores or metaphysical bookstores.)

During break times, it's a wonderful idea for Incarnated Elementals to walk outdoors, even in inclement weather. Elementals need fresh air more than any of the other realms; and those who work in industrial areas devoid of trees and grass can spend time looking at the cloud formations, since Elementals need visual contact with the beauty of the great outdoors. Nature and the outdoors is their church—it's where Incarnated Elementals feel closest to God.

An Incarnated Elemental named C.C. says: "I get so energized and refreshed in any woodsy, watery spot. I sit under a tree and can feel the good earth energy come right up through my root chakra. I feel safest when I can truly be myself without any interruptions except the gentle touch of a breeze or the sound of birds singing their melodies. The scent of the forest seems to empower me and gives me a natural high. I feel like I can conquer all when I'm there. It's a communion with nature at its best. The warmth of the sun is so healing. It's so special and such a privilege to have nature share her wealth of knowledge with me. I'm able to forget all those mundane, everyday things. I can regroup and recenter. You just can't get that in a populated area, not even in my sacred garden place at home. It's not the same."

Most Incarnated Elementals surveyed could point out specific natural environments where they wanted to live, while the other realms were more flexible about what type of area they resided in. Almost all of the Incarnated Elementals remarked, "I *have* to live in the desert," "I *must* be near the ocean," "I *need* to live in the country," and so forth.

As mentioned earlier, Incarnated Elementals prefer the company of animals, plants, flowers, or nature to that of other people. One Incarnated Elemental recalled her childhood: "I never was the popular one, that's for sure. I loved nature and animals and still do. I spent hours playing under the 17 spruce trees that lined our property. I even counted them every day to be sure they were always there. I preferred nature in my play. I loved babbling brooks and jumping from stone to stone."

Deep down, Elementals are angry at people for being so unkind to the earth and so passive about its cleanup. The exception is if they find an understanding and playful companion, often in the form of another Incarnated Elemental.

Since Elementals decide to incarnate to wield more power in helping the plant, mineral, and animal kingdoms, their life purposes almost always involve environmentalism or animal rights. This might mean teaching these values to others; or through direct involvement in campaigns, research, care, or cleanup.

In fact, it's important for Incarnated Elementals to get involved in some environmental or animal-rights cause or occupation to feel meaning in life. In addition, Elementals feel best about themselves if they take personal steps toward bettering the environment, such as recycling, or using Earth-friendly cleaning products found in health-food stores.

When I asked one Incarnated Elemental what she considered her life purpose to be, her reply reflected many of the Elementals I've met and interviewed: "My mission is to teach people about protecting the earth and the creatures who live here. I see difficulty for the planet because of man's greed and self-importance. We must do all we can to save the plants and animals before it's too late. So much has been lost. So much is in danger. Many of our fellow creatures are running out of time because of man thinking that he's better than the other creatures. If we continue to bulldoze and build, throw away and exterminate, we won't be thanked for the wasteland that's left."

Every Earth Angel realm displays high levels of creativity. It's logical, then, that Incarnated Elementals make artistic objects from nature. One Incarnated Fairy told me, "I enjoy using flower pods, leaves, pinecones, nuts, and dried flowers to make decorations and ornaments. I've made miniature habitations and furniture outdoors for the little people since I was a child."

Fiercely Protective of Nature

Since the Elementals are God's nature angels, it's no surprise that Incarnated Elementals become almost maniacally protective of animals, plants, soil, and water. Many of the Incarnated Elementals surveyed for this book told me that they had risked personal injury or retaliation in order to protect an animal, tree, or other element of nature:

E.J. writes: "I get angry when others disrespect Mother Earth and her creatures. If, while driving my car, one of my friends throws a cigarette out the window, I pull the car over and make them pick up their cigarette and dispose of it the right way."

Devon (not her real name) recalls: "I was sitting in my beautiful office one sunny day, which has floor-to-ceiling picture windows. I was staring out at the lovely trees, bushes, and rolling hills just beyond the parking lot, and I noticed a strange pickup truck pulling up. A man who didn't work in our building had stopped in our lot to eat his lunch. That was not a problem.

"However, when he threw his tall plastic beverage container into a flowering bush near his truck, it *was* a problem. When I saw this, some type of primal rage boiled in me (I'm normally a quiet, calm, laid-back person). I grabbed a co-worker and hissed, 'Come outside with me!' I guess I wanted moral support for what I was about to do.

"I ran out to the guy's truck, yelling, 'What kind of person are you to throw trash into a bush?!' He just sneered at me. I ran down the brush-covered slope (with bare legs) and retrieved the cup, scratching my legs all the while. In a moment of unbridled anger, I threw the cup into the open window of his truck, and yelled at him to leave immediately or I'd call the police. He screeched out of the parking lot, screaming foul epithets at me as he drove away.

"My co-worker just looked at me in shock, as she'd never seen me act this way in the five years she'd known me. She said, 'That's crazy. He could have pulled out a gun and shot you.'

"I realized that she was right, but I didn't care. I would not allow my friend, the flowering bush, to be treated in that way—not while I was a witness to it."

Pamela recalls: "Around the age of 19, I became aware of being one with nature. I had sprayed a bee caught in the windowsill with window cleaner and was suddenly struck by the thought, *What right do I have to kill it?* I immediately took the bee outside to the front of the house, laid it on the ground, and began to rinse it off with water. My mother thought I was crazy, leaning reverently over a dead bee, trying to resuscitate it. From that point on, I didn't kill bugs anymore. Recently, I gently swept up a swarm of ants in my apartment with a broom and put them outside. Then I politely requested that the ants no longer return, and a week later they stopped coming."

The Different Types of Elementals

As mentioned earlier, Incarnated Elementals look just like their counterparts in the spiritual Elemental world. They are larger versions of fairies, pixies, leprechauns, and so on. Here are some examples of the various types of Elementals:

— **Fairies:** Jenny is five feet tall, with a slim figure, a pretty face, large eyes, and long wavy hair that falls to her lower back. Everything about her screams, "Fairy!" and Jenny looks like she could be a model for fairy paintings and statues. She is also sweet, unassuming, and shy—just like a fairy. In fact, Jenny is so connected with the fairy realm that she gives professional angel and fairy readings, often using my *Healing with the Fairies Oracle Cards*. She advises her clients to spend time in nature to recharge their energy, and adds, "Remember to call on the angels and fairies continually to help you with every aspect of your life and mission. Also, take yourself lightly—don't get too serious! Ask the fairies to help you add enchantment and magic to your everyday experiences and your life in general."

— **Pixies, elves, and brownies:** Evie is a professional singer/songwriter with a ski-slope nose and short dark hair. She says, "People say I look like a pixie. My nicknames when I was young were, 'Tinkerbell,' 'Twinkletoes,' and 'Teensy.' I constantly have people come up to me after I've finished singing and tell me they think I'm a pixie, so I think I must be."

— **Unicorns:** Brian (not his real name) has a protruding jaw, prominent cheekbones, large eyes, and a chiseled face, like an Arabian horse. Reminiscent of a unicorn's mane, Brian dresses in long, flowing shirts untucked from his pants, and prefers his hair to be on the longer side. If you look closely at Brian, you can see or feel a beautifully braided unicorn horn protruding from his forehead. In psychic readings, clairvoyants tell Brian that his spirit guides are unicorns. This doesn't surprise him, as he has always felt an affiliation with this remarkable beast. In fact, Brian has many items that sport unicorn images. His personality is that of a hunter—he goes after spiritually based opportunities and relationships, and magically manifests new doors opening for himself. Brian says that he knows he's an Incarnated Unicorn—the message was given to him by his own guides and angels long ago.

— **Incarnated animals:** Barbara considers herself to be an "incarnated cat." She says, "I feel a camaraderie with cats and plants, and my hair has been a sexy silver color since I was a young woman of 20. I'm surrounded by lots of pet cats, and I communicate with felines and plants wonderfully. I don't especially *like* people, but will help when needed as long as they don't infringe on my quiet, private time. I have always been a cat. I worship cats and believe that if the energy in the Universe has some type of form, it would be a wonderful cat-being. Like a cat, I'm able to tell if a person is going to perform evil acts—perhaps not specifically what the acts are, but I can feel at the first meeting if a person has evil or honorable intentions. I want to tell the world that we have to respect one another, the animal-beings, and especially our Earth Mother . . . the environment."

— **Incarnated crystals:** Not to be confused with the "Crystal Children," who are highly sensitive and psychic youths, Incarnated Crystals are souls who previously inhabited the energy of crystals, boulders, and other mineral elements of the earth. Incarnated Crystals feel very connected to Mother Earth, rocks, and crystals. They love to hike and spend time outdoors, and they're very protective of the rock and soil environment.

Life-Path Work for Incarnated Elementals

Incarnated Elementals do well in artistic or media-related careers, including music, film, comedy, writing, publishing, dance, and yoga. Because they tend to be optimistic and are wonderful manifesters, they also make powerful motivational speakers. Incarnated Elementals love an audience and do well teaching groups of people. They also enjoy nature-related jobs, such as petsitting or grooming; gardening and nursery work; conservation; and forestry.

Guidance and Suggestions
If You're an Incarnated Elemental

— **Spend a lot of time in nature.** As I've emphasized repeatedly in this chapter, it's essential for Incarnated Elementals to be outdoors regularly, regardless of the weather. So, if this is your realm, take off your shoes and stockings and walk on the grass or soil every day as a way of staying grounded and connected to the earth.

— **Laugh and play.** Elementals who don't play often become depressed. So, look for ways to be silly, have fun, and laugh daily.

— **Manifest consciously.** See yourself as healthy, fulfilled, abundant, and loved. Call upon your counterparts in the spiritual Elemental kingdom to help you manifest your desires.

— **Don't throw fireballs.** Elementals' tempers are legendary, and Incarnated Elementals are no exception. When you throw a fit of rage, be careful, because you're literally throwing fireballs of hot emotion!

These fireballs can cause the objects of your wrath emotional or physical pain. Your power is like a volcano when you erupt, so please use caution. Plus, the energy can boomerang and cause painful effects for you. If you find that you've inadvertently thrown a fireball, extinguish its power immediately by calling upon the spiritual Elementals' help.

— **Detox.** You're more effective at manifesting with the high, stable energy of sobriety. You'll also feel happier and healthier with a detoxified mind and body.

— **Engage in environmentalism.** Volunteer your time or give donations to charities involved in cleaning the earth or helping animals. Recycle religiously, and spend the extra money for nontoxic cleaning chemicals and environmentally friendly products.

CHAPTER FOUR

Starpeople

*H*ollywood films and sensationalistic books portray extraterrestrials as vicious warmongers. Yet, to ETs, Earthlings are the ones who are violent—so violent, in fact, that many ETs were asked to take on human bodies to try to avert mass destruction. We call these benevolent helpers *Starpeople* (or, the singular *Starperson*).

Thank God for Starpeople. They came from physical and nonphysical galaxies and took on Earthly lives to spread kindness on an "as-needed" basis. Their collective niceness helps to defuse the anger, stress, and rage that could lead to nuclear war. If Earth is destroyed, the negative effects will ripple through many galaxies. The Starperson's assignment, then, is to prevent nuclear war at any cost. The main avenue for this lofty goal is through the expression of kindness and common decency to others—a domino effect of sorts.

On any given day, Starpeople calmly smile as they perform unselfish deeds for those on their path. Those whom they help barely notice them, yet Starpeople don't perform acts of service in order to gain accolades. Such deeds are an innate necessity to them—as if some sort of inner programming compels them to act. They aren't concerned that people rarely thank them.

Starpeople are in any place where kindness is needed. They are grocery-store checkers, postal clerks, bank tellers, and customer-service agents. With their wallflower looks and personalities, Starpeople prefer to stay "behind the scenes." Their mission doesn't call for high visibility. Quite the contrary: Starpeople are "undercover do-gooders" who hope no one notices them.

This is the first Earthly life for many Starpeople. And because this planet is so violent, emotionally and physically, Starpeople often feel overwhelmed and wish to return home. After all, Earth is one of the most turbulent planets in the Universe, and, in fact, the Universal powers have us quarantined so that we won't harm other planets. Earth is considered as dangerous as a teenager on steroids wielding a loaded gun.

Since it would upset most people to receive intervention from ETs—no matter how benevolent they might be—these mighty and gentle beings elected to take human form and walk among us. On the inside, they're the same as anyone else: beautiful sparks of Divine light made from the same Creator. Yet, because they've spent their lifetimes in non-Earthly locales, Starpeople may seem odd in behavior or looks.

Socially awkward due to their inexperience with Earth life, Starpeople may feel rejected by others. Many of the Starpeople interviewed for this book reported a history of being viciously teased in childhood, and sometimes in adulthood as well.

These experiences make the Starperson especially homesick for a planet where they fit in and know the rules of social engagement. Starperson Linda recalls, "When I was a teenager, I used to sit in my front yard and pray for a UFO to come and take me away, to take me home."

In a similar vein, Starperson Scott says, "Metaphorically, I've had my bags packed and have been ready to go home all my life. I'd prefer to work from the other side as a guide. I can remember being on another planet before coming here and being asked to participate in this planet's current drama."

Starpeople often have distinctive physical characteristics that set them apart. Rarely average height, most male Starpeople are tall and thin, with the female Starpeople being small in stature, with either thin or heavyset bodies. Of course, there are exceptions, but in general, the Starpeople's bodies—like their lives—are usually out of the norm in both height and weight.

Starpeople's faces can be long and thin, especially if they have tall, slender bodies. Starpeople who are petite have rounder faces. It appears that the planet of origin may influence their specific physical characteristics.

> *Starpeople have unusual looking eyes, such as an exotic iris color, or uncommonly shaped eyes or eyelids.*

Across the board, Starpeople have unusually shaped and colored eyes. It's common for Starpeople to have crescent-moon–shaped eyes, like an inverted U. Their eyes are often gray, green, or black-brown, and seem to glow from within, as if they have bright lights behind them. Starpeople may also have rings of lighter color around their pupils.

Since Starpeople don't like to call attention to themselves; they dress for comfort and practicality, instead of for fashion or show. Female Starpeople wear a minimum of makeup and don't like to fuss with their hair. Even a Starperson surveyed who's a professional hairdresser told me that she doesn't spend much time on her own hair color or style!

Starpeople have paradoxical personalities: On the one hand, they're eager to assist people without being asked, yet they also seem guarded and distant and may be perceived as "cold." They're here to be helpful, without needing to get deeply involved in the process of feelings and emotions, which are foreign to them. Completions of tasks are more important to them than relationship development.

Starpeople love technology, and they're usually the first to own (or invent) the latest devices. They collect state-of-the-art mobile e-mail and telephone units, along with other technological gadgets. Part of their collective soul purpose is to further technological ingenuity, for the advancement of science and humankind.

Interestingly, there aren't as many famous people who are Starpeople because of their love of staying behind the scenes. A Starperson would be more likely to direct a movie than star in it. Yet, Oprah Winfrey and Keanu Reeves are reputed to be Starpeople with high-minded purposes who are using the media as their vehicle to teach. Many believe that the film *The Matrix*, starring Reeves, contained a timely message warning us of technological dependency.

Many Starpeople wonder what their life's purpose is and are relieved to find out that it involves being helpful on an ongoing and nonspecific basis—in other words, to help in whatever way is necessary. There is no one specific "job" or "task" that they need to perform during their lifetimes as long as they're doing their best to transform human frowns into smiles.

Starperson Kath says, "It feels as if I was placed here to be available for helping anyone or anything that needs my assistance. Not a day goes by without someone needing my help in one form or another. It has been frustrating because I've never felt like I had a 'true purpose.'" Kath was relieved to discover that her continual acts of kindness and helpfulness *do*, in fact, represent her purpose.

Connections with Home

Most Starpeople have interests in UFOs, life on other planets, space travel, and ETs. They love the *Star Trek* TV series (both old and new versions), works of science fiction, and anything else that relates to these themes and topics. They completely relate to the movies *K-Pax* and *Man Facing Southeast*, two films about Starpeople in human bodies who were diagnosed as delusional because they spoke the truth about their non-Earthly origins and were put into mental institutions.

As children, Starpeople find that they have an intuitive understanding of spirituality. Many of them eschew traditional religion because it seems too restrictive compared to their understanding of the vastness of Spirit. Starperson Terry says, "I always thought of God as a Universal Intelligence that is way bigger than what conventional churches made claim to." This wisdom was most likely gained from many lifetimes of high-level awareness and experience.

Many Starpeople recall being, or believe that they were, aboard a spacecraft in this lifetime. Several of the Starpeople surveyed even knew their planet of origin. Of course, this isn't material normally discussed in polite company. Remember that these are very ordinary-looking people who know that they aren't from Earth. They're everyone's next-door neighbors, co-workers, and such, which makes reading their stories even more fascinating. Here are a few of them:

— **MaryKay:** "Through guided visualization, I was taken on a trip to find my home. Jesus came forth as my guide. We went deep into the earth, then all of a sudden, we were up in the sky. We ended up at a really bright star, so bright that I couldn't see anyone. There, I felt the love I'd been searching for my entire life. When I asked where I was, I immediately heard the word *Sirius* . . . and I had never heard that word, or that star, before."

— **Linda:** "I've always felt like I came from Pleiades. I don't even know how to spell it. As to why I feel like I come from there, I don't know why. It's just a feeling I have."

— **Scott:** "I know that I spent my last lifetime on a planet call Zeron. As best I can recall, I tended the forests there. I had a rather large head and was very tall. It was a planet to go rest and relax between lessons. It was very beautiful and green, quite lush. I was having a good time there."

Beings who live on other planets have much longer life expectancies than Earth beings. This is due to physiological differences in their bodies. In addition, they don't undergo the stress, pollution, and toxic diets that create wear and tear on Earthly bodies. Actually, many ETs have nonphysical bodies on other planets because that's what's best for their mission at that time. But the main reason why beings on other planets have extended lives is that the longer someone lives, the more can be learned.

So, a lifetime on another planet might equate three or four lifetimes here on Earth. That's why some Starpeople choose to have two or more Earthly lives during their "assignment" here. They're still Starpeople because most of their souls' history has been spent on non-Earthly soil.

When Starpeople undergo a past-life regression, the memories may not be their own. Author and past-life regressionist Dolores Cannon made this remarkable discovery while working with a client named Phil. During regressions, Phil recalled various Earthly lives. Then he remembered being on a planet quite different from Earth.

Through a series of regressions, Dolores found that this was actually Phil's first lifetime on Earth. However, he "borrowed" past-life memories from a sort of spiritual library. These borrowed memories of other Earthly lives helped to insulate and buffer Phil as he adapted to the harsh and dense Earth environment. Without these past-life memories, the violence, competition, and greed would have shocked Phil's system. Dolores writes about Phil and his experiences as a Starperson in her brilliant book, *Keepers of the Garden* (Ozark Mountain Publishing).

Even though many Starpeople feel abandoned by their home planets, as if they were dropped off here on Earth without any say in the matter, they still retain connections to home. It's common for Starpeople to have ETs as their spirit guides. They also have etheric cords reaching to starships. And Starpeople frequently soul-travel to their home planets or starships during dreamtime or meditative sojourns.

Energy Work and Sensitivity

All of the Earth Angel realms report extreme sensitivity to energy from crowds, people, and places. Yet, the Starpeople realm is the most apt to study energy healing and make a career of it. In fact, it's amazing how many Starpeople make a living using their hands, whether through energy work or via tactile occupations such as landscaping, construction, hairstyling, manicuring, massage, and assembly-line labor.

Reiki seems to be the number-one choice for energy healing work among Starpeople. This may be because Reiki energy originated from the Pleiades as a gift to Earth beings. It's interesting that Reiki energy clairvoyantly looks like thin bands of rainbow stripes, and this is also how the auras of Starpeople appear (which are visible on aura photos). They look like poles sticking vertically out of the Starperson's body, like hairs standing on end.

Starpeople are very attracted to symbols, codes, hieroglyphics, and sacred geometry, so it makes sense that they would adopt Reiki, since this healing method involves coded symbols that vibrate with different healing energies.

Toward the end of my Angel Therapy Practitioner certification courses, the students gather into groups corresponding to their respective Earth Angel realms. They then spend time together with other realm members, comparing notes about their similarities, and generally bonding with like-minded souls. I'll often interview the realm members to show patterns among them. During a recent course, every single person from the Starperson realm was also a Reiki master!

Starperson Terry says, "I am super-sensitive to energy. When I do Reiki, I can feel the shift of energy, and it pulls my hands where they should be for releasing the negative energies. Energy feels thick to me, like I'm pushing gum around."

And Starperson Nancy says, "When I do healing work, my hands heat up tremendously. I can feel the heat in a problem area on the person I'm working on."

Starpeople and Relationships

Starpeople may be born to non-Starpeople parents. These parents might not even be from any realm of the Earth Angels. As a result, the family isn't able to relate to the Starperson child, and the boy or girl ends up feeling disconnected from the birth family. Starperson Kathy recalls, "As a child, I constantly felt alone and different, even though I had five siblings."

Indeed, most planets don't have the birth and family systems of Earth life. Elsewhere, it's common for beings to be birthed in laboratories, à la the "test-tube baby" process. The emotional bonding that occurs in families here on Earth is alien to other planets as well. This is one reason why Starpeople may be perceived as friendly but distant. They're helpful, yet there's a certain degree of underlying coldness that's evident if someone attempts to create a close bond. You just never feel like you completely connect with a Starperson. And no wonder: Starpeople are task oriented, not relationship oriented. They have a job to do, and they aren't geared toward making relationships their top priority.

Starperson Scott says, "Realizing that I was a Starperson was a validation that has helped me to accept some of my colder traits, and the distance I sometimes feel toward others."

Starperson Terry has had a similar realization: "I'm different in a way that many don't understand. I feel like an outsider and very much of a loner. Most of the time, I'd rather be alone than with a group of people and their issues."

Being with other Starpeople is a way to feel accepted. Linda says, "My husband is a Starperson like me, and because of this, we connect 100 percent."

Linda's husband is 12 years younger than she is, and it seems that many female Starpeople have relationships with younger men. Typically, female Starpeople say, "I know that this man is from my home planet." Sometimes this age difference interferes with building a fully committed love relationship. It seems that male Starpeople may have come to Earth several years after the females.

When Starpeople do marry, they have very few children. Many Starpeople skip having children altogether. Linda says, "I'm 50 years old and have had a hysterectomy, so I won't be having any children. I always knew I wouldn't have kids—actually, I just didn't care either way. If my husband wanted some, fine. If he didn't, that was okay, too. But somehow I just *knew* I wouldn't bear children." Starperson Terry says that she's never been interested in what she calls "conventional family dynamics."

Starpeople often have C-section births. Perhaps that's because on other planets, vaginal births are unheard of, since babies are "bred" in laboratories. In fact, many planets' inhabitants are androgynous, without clear gender distinctions. Extraterrestrial babies aren't created through the Earthly methods of sexual intercourse, sperm, and eggs, but through a transfer of energies and the intention to create—a method portrayed in the movie *Cocoon*.

Starpeople may have made a "contract" to *not* get married or have children while living an Earth life. They probably had no prior experiences with family and love relationships and didn't even think to put marriage and children into their Earth-life contract! Having a family may interfere with the Starperson's mission, and create karma that could keep them mired in Earth's reincarnation cycles.

Also, this may be the first lifetime that a Starperson has a clear-cut gender. The female may feel uncomfortable in her woman's body, and the male may feel like an awkward imposter posing as a man. Yet, when Starpeople get to Earth and see happy couples walking arm in arm, they may wish to share in that experience. Some Starpeople are able to manifest marriage and family, while others find that this type of union perpetually eludes them.

Handling Earth Life

As mentioned earlier, Starpeople are extra sensitive to violence. All of the Earth Angel realms report an aversion toward violence and conflict. However, of all the realms, Starpeople seem to be the most repulsed by fighting in any form. Linda says, "I can't tolerate violence in the least. I can't stand it when people even raise their voices. It's almost unbearable for me. It usually brings me to tears when someone scolds me." Most Starpeople surveyed told me that they don't watch, listen to, or read the news because it upsets them too much.

The Starpeople see an eventual end to violence . . . if peace-loving men and women will take a stance in the form of prayer or guided action. In the meantime, Starpeople stay faithfully at their Earthly posts, being nice guys and gals in everyday situations. Yet, deep down, they're homesick for the peaceful life they once knew in a faraway place.

Starpeople who have learned how to handle Earth life say that it helps to connect with others in their realm. They're not difficult to spot if you look for their telltale physical characteristics. Or, you can be sure to find them near the ocean. Every single Starperson surveyed said that living near water, especially the ocean, was a *must.* A high percentage of the scuba divers I've met are Starpeople, who escape from the everyday world by spending time underwater.

MaryKay explains this connection with Starpeople and water: "I realized that I need to live near a body of water to get balanced. I go there to feel the power of this huge body of water and the waves, and it's like a battery recharge for me." And, of course, Starpeople tend to frequent UFO conventions and science-fiction study groups.

Here are some other comments from Starpeople:

— **Starperson Linda says:** "My advice to other Starpeople is that it's okay to feel like you don't belong here on Earth . . . because you don't. Just be comfortable with this fact. You're special because you came here to assist this planet with accomplishing peace. You're on this planet by choice, to heal."

— And Scott's advice for Starpeople is: "Find others to connect with who share your common views, and keep smiling at all the insanity you're surrounded with. Teach tolerance and patience and especially love, because that's all there really is. And remember, this is only a temporary assignment!"

Life-Path Work for Starpeople

Starpeople are multitaskers and may not settle on one particular career as their life's mission. They may, instead, dabble with several careers consecutively or simultaneously. Starpeople make wonderful Reiki masters, energy healers, massage therapists, chiropractors, and physical therapists. They also enjoy research, engineering, technology, and support-staff work. However, the Starpeople must believe in the goals of the company they work for or they'll be miserable in their jobs. Starpeople are kind, hardworking, and efficient, yet often perceived as being aloof or cold. They also prefer to be behind the scenes. Therefore, they're better off doing solo work than being a spokesperson or a front-office employee.

Guidance and Suggestions
If You're a Starperson

— **Know that small acts of kindness *do* count.** As a Starperson, you probably worry about Earth's future, or whether you're doing "enough." You'll feel better by remembering that the thousands of seemingly small acts of kindness you do add up to a huge contribution toward creating a peaceful planet.

— **Seek out other Starpeople.** It's essential to hang with like-minded folks. If you'll hold the intention of meeting other Starpeople, you'll soon easily attract them into your life. You can also meet Starpeople on Internet message boards and chat rooms or events with extraterrestrial themes.

— **Appreciate your uniqueness.** Your natural inclinations run counter to many Earthlings. Your standard of beauty is based more on what's on the inside than the outside—the opposite of many humans. Your priorities are more task oriented than relationship focused. So, Starperson, please honor your uniqueness, stand firm in your beliefs, and don't water down your capabilities by trying to conform.

CHAPTER FIVE

The Wise Ones: Reincarnated Sorceresses, High-Priestesses, Sorcerers, Wizards, Shamans, and Witches

Intense. Exotic. Eccentric. The Wise Ones glow from the inside. They look like romance-novel characters, usually with long, silky hair; oval faces; and haunting eyes complete with a lifetime of shadows beneath them. Earth Angels from this realm possess profound wisdom and are highly intuitive. Their eyes are penetrating, and there's no point in pretending or lying to Wise Ones, because truth is apparent to them. Eccentric and flamboyant, Wise Ones love to dress in flowing garments reminiscent of romantic eras in the past. There's a certain element of mystery accompanying each member of this

realm. It's obvious, when first meeting the gaze
of Wise Ones, that they *know*.

> When you look into the eyes of
> a Wise One, you see deep wisdom,
> knowingness, and often sorrow from
> witnessing the history of Earth and
> humanity. They may also have well-earned
> bags or shadows beneath their eyes.

The Wise Ones are humans with past lives
in which they learned how to channel their
power into miraculous healings and manifestations, including the ability to affect the
weather and material objects (through levita-
tion and telekinesis, and so on). These are the
extremely powerful and well-trained magi-
cians of the human race who were called out
of "retirement" from the spirit world in order
to come back to Earth for the currently urgent
situation on our planet.

Their energy is darker and heavier than the other Earth Angel realms. Wise Ones have a somber, serious, almost depressed energy, and they're sometimes quite stern. In relationships, they're highly opinionated in a helpful way. They're the "stage moms" and directors of their friends and family members, always knowing the best route for others to take. If someone wants solid advice, they should ask a Wise One.

Whereas the other realms are new to being human (or have past lives where they were Incarnated Angels, Elementals, and so on), the Wise Ones have been human for eons. Like the other Earth Angels, they feel "different." In fact, some Wise Ones proclaim, "I *am* different, and proud of it!" As one Incarnated Sorcerer put it: "In childhood, I realized I was different and didn't fit in, and that created difficulty—until I finally realized that my uniqueness was a benefit. I wasn't part of the mass or the norm; and when I matured, I realized that this was positive."

For that reason, the Wise Ones are more comfortable with Earth life than those in other realms. They're realistic, compassionate, and patient with people, and they've learned to enjoy their time here. Wise Ones aren't afraid to look at the shadow side of life like the other Earth Angel realms are. Incarnated Sorceress Linda spoke for many Wise Ones when she said, "I know I'm different from other people, but I don't really feel like an outsider because I basically don't care if most people like me or not." This detachment from other people's opinions is a hallmark of the Wise Ones.

The History of the Wise Ones

The common denominator of Wise Ones is the number of years they've logged learning to harness their magical powers. Some developed their own interest in metaphysics, and others were handpicked as children and schooled in the psychic arts. The Wise Ones have lived as High-Priests and Priestesses in Atlantis, ancient Greece, and Egypt; during Arthurian times; among the Mayans, as Essenes; and as native medicine men and women. They've witnessed civilizations destroyed, and people murdered for their spiritual beliefs. The Wise Ones know and appreciate the innate darkness within the human ego, but they have an even greater appreciation and respect for the heights of which humans are capable. And this is what they've come back to teach.

On the other side, many Wise Ones were comfortably enjoying the afterlife plane. They'd created paradise-like communities in the spirit world, complete with castles, gardens, and waterfalls. Everything seemed wonderful. But then the Wise Ones were approached by a committee of guides that was trying to enlist retired "spiritual soldiers" back into service. They asked the Wise Ones to return to Earth to teach and model peacefulness, and to remind people how to use their inner power and strength to create harmony.

Some Wise Ones reluctantly agreed to return to Earth. When they got here, they felt the heavy density of the shifting energy. A few Wise Ones, unable to handle this climate, exited immediately by willing their own deaths. Other Wise Ones relegated themselves to an Earth life, but felt depressed or angry about it.

The best-adjusted Wise Ones were those who resumed the study of Earth-based spirituality—such as astrology, Wicca, kabbalistic magic, Hermetics, paganism, rituals, crystal healing, herbology, candle invocations, shamanism, and so forth.

Grethel says that one of the reasons why she believes she is a Reincarnated Sorceress is "because of my early interest in chants, herbs, magic wands, and the apparatus of ritual (candles, incense, water, and so on). I also had an 'imaginary friend' as a child who was a wizard. If that weren't enough, my great aunt called me a 'sorceress' when I was young."

Members of the Wise Ones realm have spent lifetimes developing their spiritual and magical gifts. They're well practiced in the spiritual arts of manifestation, alchemy, and healing. They're born as psychic children who may view their gifts as being curses, especially if they're prescient about a forthcoming "negative" situation. The children may blame themselves for not diverting a tragedy, since they foresaw it. Yet, these psychic insights are often an opportunity for the individuals to pray about it. If they were supposed to intervene, they would have been clearly told what to do to prevent the situation.

The majority of Wise Ones whom I interviewed had vivid memories of past lives where they were witches, wizards, priests, and the like. Most of the Wise Ones surveyed had strong emotional reactions to the era of "witch burnings" from the years 1300 to

1700. Many of them have full or fragmented memories of being burned, hanged, or otherwise killed for their spiritual differences. Sara, for example, says, "I have memories of being burned at the stake while people screamed and cursed at me. I remember being viciously tortured."

The "Witch-Burning Craze" consisted of a mass superstition that anything bad—whether spoiled crops or sick children—was caused by a witch's spells. It was decided that the only way to purge this "evil" was through the burning of the witch's blood. Many of the witches were hunted by their neighbors, local governments, and churches. In more humane situations, they were killed before being tied to a pole and set on fire. Yet, in France, Germany, and Switzerland, most witches were burned alive.

Even those who weren't actually killed have conscious memories of this time period. They remember being afraid of the Inquisition, the Knights Templar, the Cathar trials (the Cathars were a pagan group in 13th-century Europe who were targeted by Pope Innocent III and were hunted and put to death), and the other various ways in which the witchhunts manifested. The threat of death hung over everyone during those times, and the memory makes Wise Ones nervous about fully reopening their spiritual gifts.

As a result, many Wise Ones hold back from unleashing their great power because of these ancient memories! Yet, the reason why they've elected to be here at this time is to teach and use those spiritual tools. A Wise One's purpose involves dusting off their psychic and spiritual healing abilities. And since we can only feel happy and fulfilled if we're engaged in our purpose, then it's necessary for Wise Ones to open and redevelop these gifts.

The Wise Ones have a special affinity with the Elemental kingdom and vice versa. Not only do fairies and elves play a role in Earth-based spiritual practices, but deep friendships were forged between the Elementals and the Wise Ones. In ancient times, people recognized the benefits of working with the Elemental kingdom, yet the churches felt threatened by this power outside of their walls. So, a negative public-relations campaign against fairies, elves, and other Elementals was waged. To this day, many people are afraid of the beautiful Elementals.

Because the Elementals were so tied in with the Wise Ones in ancient and modern times, some Incarnated Elementals may believe that they're actually from the Wise Ones realm. That's due to the shared experiences and memories of these two realms. So, a female Incarnated Elemental may remember the witch burnings—not because she was burned, but because she witnessed this happening to her Wise One friends. She may be confused and think that these are *her* memories of being burned.

Yet, the differences between the two realms are clear: Wise Ones are more solemn, dark, and serious than the playful, mischievous

Incarnated Elementals. Wise Ones have long, oval faces and prefer to wear their hair long, too (even if they currently have it cut short for business reasons); while Incarnated Elementals have round faces, and often wear their hair short (except in the case of Incarnated Fairies and Mermaids). Male Wise Ones often wear their hair in ponytails or combed back with gel. Actors Johnny Depp, Della Reese, Angelica Huston, and Jimmy Smits are examples of the looks and intensity of the Wise Ones' realm.

The Wise Ones may dress eccentrically or romantically, reflecting their favorite past-life period. Female Wise Ones prefer long, flowy "goddess gowns" in dark colors, with chunky crystal necklaces. Male Wise Ones favor woven shirts in natural fabrics or Renaissance-style shirts. The men may wear spiritually significant pendant necklaces, such as Celtic crosses or Ohm insignias. Wise Ones often love to attend Renaissance Fairs in full costume, where they can relive the highs and lows of their past lives.

The Wise Ones have dragons, wizards, and goddesses as spirit guides. They're very interested in the study of ancient eras that may be regarded as mythical, such as Avalon, Atlantis, and Lemuria. They collect wizard statues; and love books and movies dealing with magical themes, such as *The Lord of the Rings* series, the *Harry Potter* books, and anything related to Arthurian times. Many Wise Ones are also history buffs.

As Incarnated High-Priestess Marlies wrote: "I love Greek and Egyptian mythology. I can easily relate to Isis in the Egyptian tradition, and I love Pallas Athena—the goddess of wisdom and war. I deeply love her stories and her support she gave to Ulysses. With great passion, I studied ancient Greek, and I relate to all the goddesses of Olympus."

Wise Ones are also highly sensitive to moon phases—physically and emotionally affected by the full- and new-moon cycles. They often engage in "full-moon ceremonies" and celebrate the equinoxes.

Patterns Among the Wise Ones

Interestingly, every Wise One surveyed knew their sun, moon, rising, and ascendant astrological signs. This was in sharp contrast to members surveyed from other realms, who often didn't even know their sun sign, and rarely knew their moon sign. Clearly, the Wise Ones are knowledgeable about astrology, and appreciative of its applications.

A high percentage of the Wise Ones surveyed had a past or current history of heart and cardiovascular health conditions. Mitral valve prolapse, high blood pressure, tachycardia, arrhythmia, heart murmurs, and heart attacks were rampant among this realm. Could this be from heartache within the realm, for loving Earth and her people so much, and watching its potential destruction? Or, is it residual pain from the witch hunts, where the Wise Ones' blood was burned and their hearts impaled with stakes?

Louise Hay says in *Heal Your Body* that the metaphysical meaning behind heart problems is "long-standing emotional problems." The Wise Ones have carried emotional pain for eons from their many Earthly lives—talk about long-standing! Other reasons for heart problems, according to Louise, include "lack of joy, hardening of the heart, and belief in strain and stress."

The Wise Ones whom I've met are intense individuals and hardworking teachers. They teach without ceasing, often by giving brief but deeply philosophical advice to people. Yet, the look in many Wise Ones' eyes reveals years of disappointment in their students. A Wise One recently told me, "If people would just take my advice, all of their problems would cease to be. I'm not being arrogant—I *just know* what would help them. Yet, most people ignore the advice and keep wallowing in their troubles." Since the Wise Ones' purpose is to teach and be way-showers, perhaps this frustration with their mission is their greatest heartbreak.

Like Elementals, Wise Ones aren't big fans of rules and regulations. However, Elementals invariably get caught when they break rules, whereas Wise Ones cast a cloak of invisibility over themselves. They rarely get caught breaking rules. When they do, Wise Ones may blame the Elementals for the infraction.

The Wise Ones in Relationships

Most Wise Ones long for a magical and mystical soul mate marriage. They may feel the elusive presence of a kindred soul whom they've known for many lifetimes. This leads to a search for the Beloved; and until he or she is found, the Wise One may choose to be romantically alone. Or worse, the Wise One may try settling for an unfulfilling relationship.

In previous lives, Wise Ones may have taken vows of chastity or celibacy. These unbroken vows can follow someone into a current life and wreak havoc. Wise One Audrey is a perfect example. She knew that she'd had past lives as a witch and also as a nun. As a witch, she was involved with pagan rituals, celebrating the earth, nature, and the human body. This often involved ceremonies with nudity and sexuality. The reigning powers at the time deemed this material focus to be heretical, and she was burned at the stake. In her next life, Audrey was a nun, where she took a vow of celibacy. Still, she retained her mystical interests and abilities. In her present-day life, Audrey continued to practice spell casting, and knew how to manifest very well. However, her sex life was stunted in a sexless relationship with an impotent husband who was too proud to take medication or get sexual counseling. We "broke" her vows of celibacy, and she was able to rekindle her sexuality.

So, Wise Ones do best in their love lives when they use their remarkable magical powers to manifest the love they seek. Even if their true Beloved is not currently incarnate and is in the spirit world between lives, Wise Ones can manifest wonderfully fulfilling love relationships with the power of their focused intentions.

Wise Ones do best when they have friends whom they respect and admire. Otherwise, the Wise One may have friends who are actually "clients." These "friendships" are one-sided, with the Wise One acting as teacher, and the friend acting as student. The Wise Ones never get a chance to discuss their own troubles because they're cast in the strong, empowered role.

Wise Ones are often accused of being know-it-alls. This accusation actually has a kernel of truth to it, because Wise Ones are tapped into the all-knowing collective unconscious. They're also highly psychic. Linda, a Reincarnated Sorceress says, "Most often, I know what people are about to say. They get irritated with me because I finish their sentences."

The Wise Ones' children may accuse them of being controlling parents—again, because of this realm's compulsion to teach. Wise Ones *can't not* teach; however, they can temper their instruction so that it's more palatable. Instead of lecturing, for example, they can create a teaching experience that's entertaining and instructive.

As with their love lives, it's important for Wise Ones to use conscious visualizations of happy, healthy relationships with friends and family. They can use that remarkable power to see themselves surrounded by strong and loving friends who help *them*.

So if you think you're a Wise One, see and feel your children appreciating your teachings. Don't worry about how these manifestations will come about. Just know that they will. And then release the visions to the Universe so that they can manifest quickly and easily.

Magical Wise Ones

If you're a Wise One, you're a highly trained magician, and if some part of your life isn't working right now, take a proactive role in healing this area. If you passively wait for the Universe to direct you, you may find yourself spinning your wheels and going nowhere. That's because Wise Ones such as yourself are co-creators, and the Universe prefers to await your wishes and to fulfill them as asked. However, Wise Ones know from experience that not everything asked for leads to happiness. For this reason, it's prudent to pray or ask for guidance *to know what to ask for*.

Faith in these abilities is crucial, even if it's just 5 or 10 percent faith. If you ask for something but harbor the fear that it might not happen, you'll block the manifestation. If you need to, you can "borrow" faith from one of your guides. Or, you can ask the Universe to clear away fears that are thwarting your full faith.

You may have, like many other Wise Ones, taken vows in your past lives as a spiritual aspirant or devotee (such as a nun or a monk). Among the most common are vows of suffering, self-sacrifice or retribution, poverty, chastity, virginity, celibacy, obedience, and silence. Unless these vows are severed, they can follow you to Earth and place barriers in your love and sexual areas, finances, and life in general. No one is truly free until these past-life vows are broken. The only healthy vows are those that *you* decide upon—the ones you make with yourself. Even then, you'll want to regularly review them to see if they're still valid.

Break these vows and their effects by strongly affirming:

> *"I hereby sever any vows of suffering, self-sacrifice, or retribution that I may have made, in all directions of time. I rescind any negative effects of these vows, now and forever."*

Then, repeat this phrase for other vows (poverty, celibacy, and so on). Since these vows often involved signing a document with your own blood, you'll need to break the vow with an even greater amount of power. It's especially powerful to light a candle (which helps us to release negativity and break up stagnant situations) and conduct the ceremony during a full moon, which is the time of releasement. Then, stand up and stamp your foot down strongly as you make each statement aloud. Really say it like you mean it when you sever those vows!

🌲 🌲 🌲

Wise Ones, always remember the power of the word. Become clear about what you desire, and then command—through words—that it happen. You are a master spell caster, both in the name of your fears *and* your heart's desires. So, you just as easily create self-fulfilling prophecies in the direction of your ego's dictates as well as your higher self. Command your ego to silence, and direct your higher self to increase the volume of its voice.

As your manifestations appear in tangible form, welcome them with open arms. Wise Ones sometimes push away manifestations for fear that they don't deserve them. Remember, though, that these manifestations are tools that help your teaching and healing practice. Your students and clients deserve to be helped by a Wise One whose material needs are met. Put all scarcity or vows of suffering behind you now, Wise One.

Life-Path Work for Wise Ones

As a Wise One, you're a natural-born leader who's respected because of your charisma, your air of confidence, the way that you carry yourself, and your personal power. People naturally respect and admire you; they're even intimidated by you. So, they feel comfortable following your lead.

Due to your many lifetimes of spiritual learning and teaching, you'd probably enjoy a career as a spiritual teacher, astrologer, psychic, spiritual healer, channeler, or oracle-card reader. Most Wise Ones don't do well as employees or followers, unless you respect your boss or leader. You would make an excellent company president or entrepreneur, especially with your organizational skills combined with your intuitive knowledge of how to improve situations.

However, you, like most Wise Ones, would feel frustrated working with unmotivated audiences or clients who won't take your advice.

Hybrids of Wise Ones

As you'll read in the next chapter, there are variations of Wise Ones blended with other realms. They include the Knights Paladin, Mystic Angels, Star Wise Ones, and Mystic Mers.

Guidance and Suggestions
If You're a Wise One

— **Honor the power of the word.** Use vigilance with your thoughts and words to ensure that they mirror what you want, not what you fear. You manifest so quickly that you can't afford to think or talk about your fears. Focus all your energies on manifesting your desires and life purpose.

— **Honor your past.** Engage in past-life regressions to clear away leftover emotions that could be holding you back today. Read books and watch movies related to your past lives.

— **Be aware of the power of your temper.** When a Wise One slings anger toward another person, it's akin to casting a dark spell. Use your power carefully; and think twice

138

before cursing someone, as this can hurt other people as well as come back to haunt you.

— **Teach what's important to you.** You're always teaching by example. One reason to pull yourself up to your highest level is to inspire others. You elected to come to Earth to teach about human potential, so it's important for you to model that in your own life.

— **Laugh and play.** Even though you have a vital mission, it's important to inject regular doses of playfulness into your life. Sincerity, not seriousness, is called for in your mission. Laughter also helps you heal any heartbreak suffered in this life or past ones.

CHAPTER SIX

Blended Realms and Hybrids: Mystic Angels, Knights, Leprechauns, and Merpeople

*D*uring my certification programs, I explain the various realms in detail. I then ask audience members to meet with members of their realm. Those who are unsure of their realm are encouraged to join each group to discover which one feels the most comfortable. People can instantly feel if they belong in a group.

Some audience members have felt that they belonged in two of the realm groups. For example, several said that they couldn't decide whether they fit better into the Incarnated Angels or the Wise One categories. I thought that they must be souls who were evolving from one realm into another, so I'd send them to the Evolvers, Shapeshifters, or Dabblers group.

Interestingly, when my son Chase was the chief registrar for my U.S. certification programs, we always had a high percentage of Elementals among the class members. I never questioned the Elemental proportions until a spiritual counselor named Betsy Brown came on board and took over Chase's position. Suddenly, the energy of our Angel Therapy Practitioner programs completely changed.

The first course that Betsy had handled had at least 50 people who felt displaced during the realms exercise. They all had the same complaint: They fit into both the Incarnated Angels and the Wise One groups. We also had virtually no Elementals in the class, whereas we'd always previously had a rowdy group of fairies and brownies in the audience.

A new realm was discovered just like that! The new students were hybrids, which we call "Mystic Angels," just like Betsy Brown. I realized that the previously high percentage of Elementals had reflected Chase's own Elemental realm. Like does attract like!

Mystic Angels

> *When you look into the eyes of a Mystic Angel, you see compassion.*

As mentioned above, the Mystic Angels are half Wise Ones and half Incarnated Angels. Mystic Angels share much of the same characteristics as Incarnated Angels, in that they're loving, helpful, and caring. Yet, since they've had several lifetimes on Earth (as Incarnated Angels), they're street-smart and edgy. They might cuss, abuse alcohol, or gamble . . . yet they're still angels.

Mystic Angels appreciate rules because they abhor chaos. Like Incarnated Angels, they'll apologize. Yet they only say "I'm sorry" because it's a fast way to clear up conflict, and not because they feel guilty. Incarnated Angels have the corner on harboring guilt feelings among the realms.

Mystic Angels have the hard-won wisdom that comes from many lifetimes of helping in the trenches of wars and conflict. Even though they've seen it all, Mystic Angels still retain faith in the goodness of humanity.

Mystic Angels aren't timid in front of audiences compared to Incarnated Angels. With their Wise One heritage, Mystic Angels make wonderful teachers, speakers, and workshop presenters. They love to teach about healing techniques and offer tips for happy living.

Mystic Angels aren't afraid to acknowledge the shadow side of life. They clearly see the ego issues behind human dramas. The focus and language of a Mystic Angel is a bit darker and earthier than that of an Incarnated Angel (which is a realm that doesn't like to look at or acknowledge problems or shadows).

One Mystic Angel described her realm's characteristics in this way: "We like to use both Angel Oracle Cards and also Tarot cards. We're healers who are know-it-alls. Because we've been killed in previous lifetimes, we're often afraid to come out of the spiritual closet. But when we do, we fly high and fast in putting our purpose into action."

Knights Paladin

This realm was uncovered by my son Grant. As you may recall, Grant was the person who originally pointed out the Wise One realm to me. After we delineated this realm, Grant saw that he actually fit into a subcategory of Wise Ones that we initially called "Knights." However, that term wasn't accurate because it implied pure warriors. So the term *Paladin* was suggested by two members of this realm. Paladin, pronounced *pal-AH-den,* refers to a magical or holy knight who crusades in the name of upholding goodness and order. Historical Paladins were wizards who cast spells to complete their missions.

Knights Paladin share many qualities with Mystic Angels in that they're half Wise One and half angel. Mystic Angels express their angelic side through healing others, either with their teaching wisdom or with their energy. Knights Paladin represent the protective guardian side of angels. Mystic Angels express the Archangel Raphael's healing energy, while Knights Paladin express Archangel Michael's sword-wielding energy.

Knights Paladin are the custodians of orderliness; and the upholders of truth, sacred secrets, and civility. They are trustworthy, able to keep secrets (unless leaking the secret would help uphold justice), and extremely helpful to loved ones and strangers. Knights Paladin feel uncomfortable in social settings, unless they're discussing a topic of personal interest. They're chivalrous and polite, yet they can also be staunch and unyielding when their values are threatened. Knights Paladin refuse to compromise when it comes to ethics. Remember that Incarnated Angels (which Knights Paladin are blended from) respect authority, organization, and rules, especially when they believe in those rules.

Members of this realm served as Knights Templar; members of the Round Table; members of the twelve *chansons de geste* of medieval legend; and bodyguards of high-priests, high-priestesses, saints, and sages. Knights Paladin tend to have large bodies and muscular strength. They stand tall with egoless pride; and their eyes are intense, clear, and focused like a bodyguard on high alert. They notice everything.

Knights Paladin have a lifelong fascination with knights, suits of armor, stories of the Round Table, dragons, and jousting. They love video games, books, and movies involving wartime strategies, sword fights, and redemption. Famous Knights Paladin include Joan of Arc, King Arthur, King David, and Sir Lancelot.

> *The eyes of a Knight Paladin are intense, clear, and focused, like a bodyguard on high alert.*

Many Knights Paladin are drawn to armed services, security, and police work, which are modern equivalents of knight orders. They also join or read about secret spiritual societies such as the Freemasons, Knights Templar, and Rosicrucians. Yet, modern-day Knights Paladin often must take solo missions to fulfill their destinies. Instead of following the King's orders, today's Knights Paladin must follow the orders of their internal guidance. So joining the military or police force may hamper the freedom to follow this inner wisdom, or could even dampen the voice itself.

Knights Paladin also have Eastern counterparts in Samurais and Shaolin Monks, who incorporate breath work, posture, self-discipline, and wisdom in their approaches to managing life.

Knights Paladin make wonderful advocates and activists who champion the causes they believe in. They do well in areas of law, politics, writing, speaking, coaching, campaigning, and leading. Knights Paladin who are Indigos (the generation of highly sensitive natural-born leaders and visionaries) can make intense and inspirational leaders.

Incarnated dragons are a subcategory of this realm.

Mystic Stars

This hybrid is a blend of Starpeople and Wise Ones. Mystic Stars are natural-born teachers who bring universal knowledge to Earth. Their teachings have the global purpose of inspiring world peace, by giving humans helpful information to reduce their stress levels.

> *Mystic Stars have very exotic, different-looking eyes that reflect their serious, somber, and intense passion for teaching.*

Mystic Stars are highly sensitive and can feel the energy of other people's emotions. They often become uncomfortable around others, and can sometimes act socially awkward. Mystic Stars combat social stress by teaching facts and philosophies.

Mystic Stars unwittingly try to teach family members whose eyes are glazed over from an overload of technical information. So, Mystic Stars do best when they pay attention to cues from their students and audience members, and watch for wavering attention levels. Mystic Stars are so intelligent that they may unwittingly talk over someone's head without realizing it. Without dumbing down their lessons, Mystic Stars can tailor their teachings so that they're more easily digestible.

Leprechauns

When we think of Leprechauns, little men in green suits come to mind. However, the Earth Angels realm of Leprechauns includes a wide variety of body shapes, sizes, and clothing styles. There are both male and female Leprechauns, and many members of this realm *do* look like giant Leprechauns. Yet, it's what's on the inside rather than outside that distinguishes this realm from the others.

Leprechauns are half Wise Ones and half Incarnated Elementals. They have the wisdom that comes from many lifetimes on earth, a down-to-earth common sense approach to life, a deep connection to nature, and a wicked sense of humor.

One minute when you look into a Leprechaun's eyes you see the serious intensity of a wise teacher. The next minute, though, you'll see the mischievous look of a seven-year-old who's about to play a prank.

To understand the Leprechaun realm, let's look at their history. One of the original peoples of Ireland were called The Tuatha de Danaans, which means "The Children of Dana" or "The People of Dana." Dana was a Celtic Creator Goddess. The Tuathas possessed magical abilities to shape-shift and time-travel and were considered demigods in some circles. They fought battles to maintain possession of Ireland, but eventually were defeated by the invading Gaels. Instead of leaving their island, though, the Tuathas shape-shifted into another dimension and became Leprechauns. Today, they still run Ireland, yet are only visible to those with open minds and hearts.

So lightworkers from the Leprechaun realm are half Wise One and half Elemental. They possess ancient knowledge about magic, healing, and manifestation like Wise Ones from other cultures. As Leprechauns, they express the Elemental characteristics of living interdimensionally, with a strong connection to nature.

Those from the Leprechaun realm show qualities of both Wise Ones and Elementals. They vacillate between serious teachers and rowdy jokesters. They lecture you one minute, and then tickle you the next. Even though we think of Leprechauns as red-bearded little men with paunches and green outfits, the members of the Leprechaun realm can look as gorgeous as fashion models. Many members of this realm do have touches of Leprechaun looks, whether it's a penchant for wearing green t-shirts, reddish hair, a ruddy complexion, or even a bit of a tummy paunch.

Leprechauns make wonderfully entertaining teachers who keep their students enthralled and interested. They're wonderful storytellers, yet their tales always have important messages. As long as you can weather their vacillating moods and occasional flirtations, Leprechauns make wonderful friends and romantic partners. You'll never be bored with a member of this realm, that's for sure!

Merpeople

> *The majority of Merpeople have green coloring in their eyes.*

Like Leprechauns, Merpeople are hybrids from the Elemental realm, so they also possess playful and mischievous sides. In my book, *Goddesses & Angels*, I published the results of my survey of Merpeople:

I selected only the surveys of those who knew that they were definitely Mer-people. Most based this opinion on the fact that they matched my descriptions, they *had* to live near water, they'd identified with mermaids or mermen since childhood, had frequent dreams about mermaids, and so on.

Of all the measures on the survey, the significant factors were:

- 82% had a natural red tint or highlights in their hair

- 82% preferred to wear their hair long (89% of just the females surveyed)

- 79% had naturally curly or wavy hair

- 69% had green in their eyes

- 85% reported being frequently or constantly thirsty for water

- 80% said they felt cold often, even in warm weather

The 82 percent of red- and auburn-haired respondents eclipses the estimated 2 to 10 percent of people with naturally red or auburn hair in the general population. Apparently, red hair is a genetic anomaly. At one time, red-haired women were accused of witchcraft. In the 16th and 17th centuries, red-headed European women were put to death during the witch-hunting crusades. Could they have been Merpeople who retained their magical abilities and knowledge?

As mentioned above, Merpeople must live near bodies of water to feel happy and healthy. Merfairies are drawn to rivers and lakes, while Merangels, Mystic Mers, and

Star-Mers feel connected to the ocean. Many Merpeople have memories of, or are attracted to stories about, Atlantis and Lemuria, which are two ancient oceanic civilizations.

As with other realms, Merpeople look like their spiritual counterparts. Female Merpeople resemble mermaids with hourglass, curvy figures and a penchant for wearing turquoise water-colored clothing. Mermen look athletic, trim, and outdoorsy. Both genders prefer wearing their hair long, and their tresses have natural waves. The majority have a naturally red tint in their hair.

Merpeople report feeling cold easily, and they prefer to vacation or live in tropical climates. As much as they love to swim, though, Merpeople avoid chlorinated swimming pools because they're sensitive to the smell and feel of chlorine.

Merpeople are frequently thirsty and many have issues with constipation. They usually have a bottle of water at hand, and they do best avoiding dried fruit, which tends to leach water out of their systems. Merpeople have dry skin on their feet, toes, and heels. Their water sensitivity also causes Merpeople to be very choosy about which brand of bottled water they drink. Merpeople often crave seaweed salad, sea vegetables, and nori (flattened seaweed wrapped around sushi rolls), probably because their bodies need the special sea-based nutrients.

Most people love dolphins, but Merpeople are fanatical about them. Merpeople also love whales, seabirds, seahorses, dragonflies, and other water-dwelling beings. Many Merpeople volunteer time or money to support charities or events that protect the oceans, lakes, and rivers. Their favorite vacation destination is a tropical beach, and they either live near a body of water or long to do so. Merpeople also diligently pick up litter from beaches and lakefronts.

There are several Merpeople subcategories, including:

— **Merangels:** As a hybrid of half Incarnated Angel and half Elemental (Mer is part of the Elemental realm), Merangels vacillate between being naughty and nice. Female Merangels may resemble Incarnated Angels, with their voluptuous bodies; heart-shaped, youthful faces; and tumbling, highlighted hair. Yet, they are the Incarnated Angels who've lived on the edge. They may have histories of drug and alcohol abuse, relationship betrayals, and even criminal records. However, their hearts are purely angelic at the core.

— **Merfairies:** This hybrid is 100 percent Elemental, so Merfairies have no apologies about being party animals at the ocean, lakes, or rivers. They enjoy cocktails while watching seaside sunsets, boating, or lazing on a beach. Merfairies may be perfectionistic about their romantic partners, which may lead to a long succession of boyfriends and girlfriends. Yet, Merfairies will tell you that they're trying to find lifelong satisfaction, in the form of a fun, financially secure—oh, and did I mention fun?— relationship. Merfairies love to camp, hike, and be next to lakes and rivers set in the mountains. They have a special bond with the water fairies, which are called "sprites," "undines," and dragonflies.

— **Star-Mers:** Starpeople love being near the ocean, but this hybrid is especially drawn to the sea. Star-Mers are loners who prefer to sail, swim, surf, scuba dive, or snorkel by themselves (or with one special and trusted companion). Star-Mers especially love to look at the starry skies while drifting on a boat in the middle of the ocean. They connect with their home planets through the energy of the water's ions.

— **Mystic Mers:** This hybrid realm is a blend of Merperson and Wise One. They have the edgy Elemental personality combined with the seriousness of Wise Ones. They love to teach, especially about dolphins, whales, Atlantis, ocean ecology, scuba diving, sailing, or any other wisdom related to the ocean.

— **Incarnated Dolphins:** This hybrid consists of dolphins who have taken on human form so that their message is clearly heard by people. Yet, their appearance belies their true identity. Incarnated Dolphins' bodies are shaped like *actual* dolphin bodies. Their slightly protruding belly casts their body in the same dimensions as an American football. Most Incarnated Dolphins have gray eyes, just like oceanic dolphins.

Most Incarnated Dolphins have gray eyes, like their oceanic counterparts.

Incarnated Dolphins also chuckle with the same snickering laugh as ocean-dwelling dolphins. Most Incarnated Dolphins have sea-related professions such as marine biologist, oceanographer, boat captain, or ocean ecologist. They're passionate about preserving the sea's ecology and make wonderful teachers in this area. Yet, because of their dolphin origin, this realm knows how to relax, play, and flirt while meeting their responsibilities. Because they're accustomed to swimming in pods, Incarnated Dolphins are usually very social. They love long and light-hearted discussions.

For example, a woman I know named Gayle loves dolphins, and regularly leads group excursions to swim with them in exotic locations. She even looks like a dolphin, with her sleekly rounded body and oval eyes. Interestingly, Gayle runs a swimming-pool company. Her sun sign is Pisces, the sign of the fish, and a water sign. She says, "I love the ocean and *have* to spend time there to recharge. I love dolphins and whales and spend much time in the ocean swimming with them. I asked my guides why I feel so connected to the ocean, and I was told, 'Because, Gayle, you are *of* the ocean.' At first, I didn't understand what that meant. Now I do believe that I may have been a dolphin before."

In addition to Incarnated Dolphins, I've also met a few Incarnated Whales and, no, they're not obese. While Incarnated Dolphins have a playful, Elemental personality, Incarnated Whales have the protective and loving energy of archangels. Incarnated Whales are fascinated with sea-dwelling whales; and often become advocates, activists, marine biologists, sailors, or scuba divers in order to spend time studying about whales.

These are the major hybrids that have been revealed to me since teaching this material to audience members. Those who can't relate to any of the realms continue to help me pinpoint other hybrids. Yet, some people just defy all realm categories. For them, we've developed other ways of looking at blended realms, as you'll read about next.

⋙ ✳ ⋘

CHAPTER SEVEN

If You Feel
That You Fit into
Several Realms . . .

*a*bout 10 percent of my audience members who hear the description of the Earth Angel realms tell me, "I feel like I fit into more than one category!" These Earth Angels know that they're lightworkers, yet they're unclear about their particular realm. Here are some points to consider:

1. Energy: Tune in to your overall "energy blueprint"

The energy of a(n):	*Is:*
Incarnated Angel	Sweet and loving
Incarnated Elemental	Warm, playful, and mischievous
Starperson	Helpful, cool, and detached
Wise One	Serious, intense, and regal
Leprechaun	Alternating serious and silly
Mystic Angel	Serious, intense, sweet, and loving

Merperson	Alternates between being rebellious and acquiescent
Knight Paladin	Attentive and polite, yet socially awkward

2. Physical appearance

People in this realm:	_Have these physical characteristics:_
Incarnated Angels	Beautiful or cherubic faces with large bodies
Incarnated Elementals	Look like larger versions of fairies, elves, sprites, and gnomes
Starpeople	Are tall and lanky; or short, with thin or large bodies.

REALMS OF THE EARTH ANGELS

They have unusual eyes and facial features. Plain in dress, they wear minimal makeup.

Wise Ones

Long faces, with faraway expressions in their eyes. They wear dark-colored flowing shirts and dresses and often have long, prematurely gray hair.

Leprechaun

Many look like leprechauns. They prefer to wear green and earth tone–colored clothing. They have a twinkle in their eyes most of the time.

Mystic Angel	An attractive face, large body, and very serious facial expression
Merperson	Females have hour-glass-like curvy bodies. Eyes tend to have green in them, and hair tends to have red in it. Male and female Merpersons prefer long hair. They often wear blue-, turquoise-, or teal-colored clothing.
Knight Paladin	Tall; large body; intense eyes

3. Interests

People in this realm:	*Focus on:*
Incarnated Angels	Healing and service work; keeping relationships peaceful and happy
Incarnated Elementals	Teaching, entertaining, the arts, and environmentalism
Starpeople	Energy healing, particularly Reiki; technological advances; being helpful as needed.
Wise Ones	Teaching; practicing mystical, psychic, and Earth-based spirituality

Leprechaun	Teaching, music, storytelling, playing practical jokes
Mystic Angel	Teaching about healing
Merperson	Dolphins, whales, water sports, the ocean, Lemuria, and Atlantis
Knight Paladin	Upholding justice, truth, and freedom; protecting "underdogs" and just causes

The Evolving Soul and the Shapeshifter

If you still don't know your realm, you may come from an as-yet-undiscovered realm. Or you may be an "Evolving Soul" or a "Shapeshifter." (We previously called the Shapeshifter group by the term *Dabblers*). That means that you're either moving from one realm to the next, or are hopscotching through the realms for the sake of variety and growth.

— **The Evolving Soul:** If you're an Evolving Soul, you're moving from one realm to the next, so you may not identify with one particular group. Perhaps you've spent many lifetimes in one realm and have learned everything you can from this experience, so you elect to enter a new realm. You don't identify fully with the group you just left or the group you're newly joining.

If this sounds like you, give yourself time to adjust to the new group, and don't judge yourself harshly for feeling disconnected. Earth Angels in the Evolving Soul category can feel doubly alienated—not only do you feel separate from humans, but you feel different from the other Earth Angels as well!

It can feel like being the last kid picked for a softball team: unwanted and unappreciated.

Know that these are temporary feelings, and pray for spiritual assistance to know that you're not alone and that you *are* wanted and appreciated. After all, you were very brave to switch to a new realm, and you probably did so out of the noble intention to be extra helpful to the world!

— **The Shapeshifter:** Some souls desire variety, excitement, and a wealth of experience. If you're a Shapeshifter, like "a kid in a candy store," you can't decide what you want, so you select everything on the menu. The Shapeshifters are Earth Angels who move from realm to realm. You never quite settle into one particular realm family. Instead, you graze from the highlights that each realm has to offer. Simultaneously, you bring gifts to each realm from the lessons you've learned while in the other Earth Angel realms. Shapeshifters rapidly adapt to new situations and people, much like children who move a lot and attend different schools, yet develop the ability to quickly fit in.

🔺 🔺 🔺

If you're an Evolving Soul or a Shape-shifter, you're like a honeybee going from flower to flower, taking and bringing nourishment as you travel. You provide valuable services because you infuse the realms with fresh blood, new ideas, and awakened vitality.

You could also be from a new realm that's yet undiscovered. As the world unfolds, new missions are required. And if you're one of the souls initiating those new missions, God bless you for your service!

Life-Path Work for
Evolving Souls and Shapeshifters

Evolving Souls and Shapeshifters fall into two distinct groups: the Independent Thinkers and the Adaptors. Independent Thinkers are take-charge individuals and radical nonconformists who take pride in being outsiders. They believe that "normalcy" is tantamount to being sentenced to mediocrity. Independent Thinkers are champions of humanitarian and environmentalist causes—unless the causes are too popular. Independent Thinkers don't like to be trendy, and they desire their own unique niche outside of the mass populace.

Independent Thinkers, not surprisingly, do best in self-employment work geared around artistic or inventive pursuits. They don't enjoy systems, rules, or guidelines from outside "authorities." Ideal careers for Independent Thinkers would be the fine arts, craftwork, publishing, writing, or photography.

Shapeshifters love any career that offers them excitement and an opportunity to learn. They're better at working with the public than the Independent Thinkers. Ideal careers would be travel (working as a tour guide or working on a cruise ship), being a talent agent or scout (making other people's dreams come true), and any sales work involving a product or service that the Shapeshifter truly believes in.

Guidance and Suggestions If You're an Evolving Soul or a Shapeshifter

— **Respect your decision for independence.** Souls in this nonrealm are generally nonconformists and rabble-rousers. The earth needs your strength and power right now, so please don't dilute it by trying to fit in to any particular group (unless it comes naturally).

— **Teach freedom.** Too many humans allow themselves to be controlled by reigning authorities. By your refusal to conform or be tied down, you teach them alternatives. The more that you can do to garner personal happiness and peace, the more effective your teachings will be. Remember that you teach first by example, and then formal teaching opportunities arise as you allow them.

— **Manifest, manifest, manifest.** Because you tend to work outside of systems, you need to rely upon your personal manifestation power to sustain you materially. Remember that there are no neutral thoughts or words, so everything you say and think creates your future. Therefore, think about what you desire, not about what you fear.

We're Counting on You!

*E*arth Angel, thank you for being on the planet at this time. With your great loving energy, you're helping us just by being here! And yet—as you're well aware—you signed up for so much more. You elected to come here at a crucial time in our planet's history to effect great change, utilizing your natural resources of talents combined with harmonious actions.

Unless the mass populace takes a different approach to the environment and each other, life as we know it may not continue. You're here to teach alternatives. You'll know what to teach by noticing which issues fuel your passions, excitement, worry, or anger.

For example, you might be here to teach us, your fellow human beings, how to manifest material needs so that we don't compete, steal, or go to war to get our share. Or perhaps you're here to teach about the vital necessity of protecting our air, water, and soil quality. Maybe you contracted to teach healthier ways to raise and educate children. There are hundreds of vital topics to teach right now.

How do you teach? In any way you can—for instance, by being a role model, authoring books, writing articles, sending letters to editors of publications, taking action within educational and government systems, and/or by giving speeches or making media appearances.

One thing is clear: We need Earth Angels who are willing to be leaders. Old systems that lack integrity are beginning to fall, such as corporations and churches with histories of abuse. The new energy will no longer support or hide dark energy. Darkness within the educational, government, and legal systems will also cause them to wobble. As these changes occur, Earth Angel leaders (such as you) can guide people away from panic and pessimism, and toward a focus on letting the old be replaced with something better.

We're all counting on you to take the reins of your life's purpose and embrace it fully. Any step that you take is helpful and sorely needed right now . . . provided that it comes from your intention to help. Please don't delay moving forward, waiting to figure out exactly what your mission is, what next step to take, or to receive an ironclad guarantee that you'll succeed. Doing *anything* that comes from love in your heart will be helpful, much like the ways in which small gifts given to a worthy cause eventually add up to a hefty donation. Start anywhere—just dive in!

Along the way, please take good care of your physical body. It's a very important tool in your mission. Yet, many Earth Angels such as yourself have never had a physical body before, so you may neglect or abuse it.

By feeding it organic foods and beverages, exercising regularly, and getting adequate rest, you'll have more energy for your life's purpose.

A number of years ago, a very influential Earth Angel named Louise L. Hay (whom I've mentioned several times in this book, and who's the founder of Hay House, my publisher) was guided to write about her insights into the link between physical ailments and underlying thoughts. Yet, not one publisher would print her materials! So instead of giving up, she typed and stapled several copies of the manuscript herself. Then, she felt urged to give workshops on the topic. At first, only two or three people came to her lectures. Today, that manuscript—*Heal Your Body*—has helped countless people, and was the basis for her *New York Times* bestseller *You Can Heal Your Life,* which has sold 30 million copies around the world. And now, when Louise gives a lecture, thousands of people attend!

Aren't you glad that Louise didn't get discouraged about her life's purpose and that she persevered? There are dozens of similar stories of people who've made the world a better place, and whose beginnings were quite humble.

🦋 🦋 🦋

Your true self is a creation of love, while your ego is a creation of fear. Your ego's goals are aimed toward making you feel small, inadequate, and powerless, yet how can a being who's made in the image and likeness of the Creator be *anything* but mighty, powerful, and wise?

Your ego knows that if you remember your true spiritual nature (perfect, powerful, creative, and intelligent), it will lose its power to frighten you, so it feeds you lies such as: "If you become powerful, you'll abuse that power. People won't like you as much. People will be jealous of you," and so on. Please, please don't listen to the ego! Tell it to go sit in the corner and keep its rantings to itself. Treat it like a buzzing fly, and don't focus on it.

The angels say, "If you get nervous, focus on service." Nervousness comes from ego concerns about other people's opinions. A focus upon "How can I bring more love and light to this situation right now?" elicits your higher self's natural spiritual gifts and power.

Remember that the bigger the purpose, the bigger the fear; there's a correlation. The more people that you'll potentially help, the more force your ego will use to hold you back. Your ego urges you to delay your mission by preparing instead of doing. Your ego says, "First you have to lose weight, make more money, get married, get divorced, move, graduate, get published, open a healing center, and so forth . . . and *then* you'll be able to help the world." That's nonsense!

Earth Angel, you're ready right now for your mission! There will never be a day more perfect than today to work on it! Even though you may feel unqualified or unprepared, do it anyway! Author Sheldon Kopp once wrote: "I have never begun any important venture for which I felt adequately prepared." In other words, you'll probably never feel completely ready for your mission, so there's no point in waiting.

Pray for daily assignments that tell you how you can help make Earth a cleaner and more peaceful environment. Your prayers will be answered in the form of opportunities for you to teach and heal. As these doors open for you, please don't turn and run the other way. You *are* ready. You *deserve* to do this beautiful work. And you *are* qualified . . . *now!*

Resources for
Earth Angels

Books for Incarnated Angels

There aren't any books that I'm aware of about Incarnated Angels (other than this book); however, here are some works that will be helpful for you if you're in this realm:

The Assertive Woman, by Stanlee Phelps and Nancy Austin (Impact Publishers, 1997)

When I Say No, I Feel Guilty, by Manuel J. Smith, Ph.D. (Bantam Books, 1975)

Your Perfect Right: Assertiveness and Equality in Your Life and Relationships, by Robert E. Alberti and Michael L. Emmons (Impact Publishers, 2001)

Support Groups for Incarnated Angels

Although the groups below aren't specifically for you Incarnated Angels, they can help you learn about assertiveness and boundaries, and give you support while you reclaim your personal power. Meetings are held throughout the world. You can get a list of these meetings by contacting:

Al-Anon
1600 Corporate Landing Parkway
Virginia Beach, VA 23454-5617
e-mail: wso@al-anon.org • **www.al-anon.org**

Co-Dependents Anonymous
P.O. Box 33577
Phoenix, AZ 85067-3577
e-mail: outreach@coda.org • **www.coda.org**

Study Groups for *A Course in Miracles*

The book *A Course in Miracles* is a wonderful resource to help you heal from guilt. You can find the book at any bookstore, or download a free copy of the original and unedited *Course* by typing in the words Urtext+A Course in Miracles using an Internet search engine (like Google).You may also find *Course* book-study groups a helpful support network. You can find a listing of study groups through:

Miracle Distribution Center
3947 E. La Palma Ave.
Anaheim, CA 92807
(714) 632-9005 • fax: (714) 632-9115
e- mail: info@miraclecenter.org
www.miraclecenter.org

Books for and about Incarnated Elementals

Summer with the Leprechauns: A True Story, by Tanis Helliwell (Blue Dolphin Publishing, 1997)

Healing with the Fairies, by Doreen Virtue, Ph.D. (Hay House, 2001)

The Elves of Lily Hill Farm, by Penny Kelly (Lily Hill Publishing, 2005)

Books about Starpeople

Aliens Among Us, by Ruth Montgomery (Fawcett Publishing, 1986)

E.T. 101: The Cosmic Instruction Manual, by Zoev Jho and Diana Luppi (Intergalactic Council Publications, 1990)

Keepers of the Garden, by Dolores Cannon
(Ozark Mountain Publishing, 1993)

The Star People, by Brad & Francie Steiger
(Berkley Publishing Group, 1986)

Starborn, by Brad Steiger & Sherry Hansen
Steiger (Berkley Publishing Group, 1992)

From Elsewhere: Being E.T. in America, by Scott
Mandelker (Carol Publishing Books, 1995)

*Universal Vision: Soul Evolution and the Cosmic
Plan*, by Scott Mandelker (U.V. Way Publishing, 2000)

Books about Merpeople

Goddesses & Angels, by Doreen Virtue
(Hay House, 2005)

About the Author

Doreen Virtue, Ph.D., is a clairvoyant metaphysician who holds B.A., M.A., and Ph.D. degrees in counseling psychology. A former psychotherapist, Doreen now gives workshops on topics related to her books and oracle cards. She's the author of *The Care and Feeding of Indigo Children,* the *Healing with the Angels* book and oracle cards, and the *Messages from Your Angels* book and oracle cards, among many other works. She has appeared on *Oprah,* CNN, and *Good Morning America;* and has been featured in newspapers and magazines worldwide. For information on Doreen's workshops, please visit her Website at: **www.AngelTherapy.com.**

We hope you enjoyed this Hay House book.
If you'd like to receive a free catalog featuring additional
Hay House books and products, or if you'd like information
about the Hay Foundation, please contact:

Hay House, Inc.
P.O. Box 5100
Carlsbad, CA 92018-5100

(760) 431-7695 or **(800) 654-5126**
(760) 431-6948 (fax) or **(800) 650-5115 (fax)**
www.hayhouse.com® • www.hayfoundation.org

Published and distributed in Australia by: Hay House Australia Pty.
Ltd.18/36 Ralph St. • Alexandria NSW 2015 • *Phone:* 612-9669-4299
Fax: 612-9669-4144 • www.hayhouse.com.au

Published and distributed in the United Kingdom by: Hay House UK,
Ltd. 292B Kensal Rd., London W10 5BE • *Phone:* 44-20-8962-1230
Fax: 44-20-8962-1239 • www.hayhouse.co.uk

Published and distributed in the Republic of South Africa by:
Hay House SA (Pty), Ltd., P.O. Box 990, Witkoppen 2068
Phone/Fax: 27-11-706-6612 • orders@psdprom.co.za

Published in India by: Hay House Publishers India,
Muskaan Complex, Plot No. 3, B-2, Vasant Kunj, New Delhi 110 070
Phone: 91-11-4176-1620 • *Fax:* 91-11-4176-1630 • www.hayhouseindia.co.in

Distributed in Canada by: Raincoast • 9050 Shaughnessy St.,
Vancouver, B.C. V6P 6E5 • *Phone:* (604) 323-7100
Fax: (604) 323-2600 • www.raincoast.com

Tune in to HayHouseRadio.com® for the best in inspirational
talk radio featuring top Hay House authors! And, sign up via the Hay
House USA Website to receive the Hay House online newsletter and stay
informed about what's going on with your favorite authors. You'll receive
bimonthly announcements about: Discounts and Offers, Special Events,
Product Highlights, Free Excerpts, Giveaways, and more!
www.hayhouse.com®